Liberating Leadership

Liberating Leadership

David Turner

The Industrial Society

First published 1998 by
The Industrial Society
Robert Hyde House
48 Bryanston Square
London W1H 7LN
Telephone: 0171 479 2000

ISBN 1 85835 525 7

Stylus Publishing Inc
22883 Quicksilver Drive
Sterling
VA 20166-2012
USA

**British Library Cataloguing-in-Publication Data.
A catalogue record for this publication is available from the
British Library.**

Typeset by: The Midlands Book Typesetting Co.
Printed by: J. W. Arrowsmith Ltd
Cover design: Jordan Design
Cover photo: KOS Picture Source

The Industrial Society is a Registered Charity No. 290003

Contents

Introduction: a new way forward in managerial leadership

Leadership has always been an essential component in the management of every effective organisation. Leadership is changing, however. What was seen as leadership behaviour twenty years ago no longer fits the bill. Members of today's workforce have different expectations from those of their parents and they are ready, willing and able to contribute much more. The traditional image of the single, strong, charismatic and domineering leader has faded: such a figure is inappropriate for the complexities of modern, internationally competitive businesses or the streamlined public sector.

Organisations cannot remain competitive if they continue to use outdated managerial methods: they can only succeed if they unlock the potential and creative energies of *all* their employees.

Today's organisation needs liberating leadership, enabling those in managerial roles to harness the skills and talents of everyone in their particular section. As liberating leaders, they create situations where continuous improvement can occur. They demonstrate, by their own behaviour, how people can be liberated to maximise their skills. They recognise the need for continuing change and urge everyone to meet the challenges that this brings, supporting and encouraging them to reach their full potential.

In a liberating environment, managers no longer have to take command and control of everything, with a responsibility for all decision-making. Instead, they must become facilitators, coaches, enablers and supporters, encouraging those closest to the tasks to take their own decisions.

Liberating leadership should be promoted at all levels of an organisation. It represents a radically new form of leadership which rejects position, status and hierarchy. In short, liberating leadership is Democracy at Work.

This book demonstrates the benefits of this new approach to leading and managing, setting out the beliefs and behaviours which you can practise in order to become a disciple of liberating leadership yourself. It contains special tips to help you brush up the enabling skills which the liberating leader needs and selected action portraits of liberating leadership in real organisations which have embraced the concept.

CHAPTER 1

Organisations, managers and leaders

Organisations

We are all familiar with organisations, because they're everywhere. No part of the fabric of a modern nation can escape them. Manufacturing industry, the wholesale and retail trades, the health services, the professions, financial services, charities and voluntary bodies, public utilities, the churches and private companies – all seek to operate through organisations.

The dictionary defines 'organisation' as *a business or administrative concern constructed and organised for a particular purpose.* The typical organisation, when first formed, was small. From early pioneering days, through uncertain times, it grew into a strong and confident concern. Many of today's large organisations have such a history.

Established organisations have survived and thrived because they have adapted themselves to meet changing needs, altering, developing or redesigning the way they are 'constructed and organised'. They have faced a sequence of different constraints and pressures which have led to constant reshaping.

> **'I never want to hear anyone saying "we've always done it this way!"'**
>
> *Managing Director*

For many organisations, competition is fiercer now than it has ever been and rapid advances in communications and information technology have globalised the domestic marketplace. Gaining and maintaining a 'competitive edge' has become the 'particular purpose' of the organisation.

The key to gaining that vital competitive edge used to lie in the investment in better equipment or new technology, but this is not necessarily the case today. Increasingly, the vital ingredient is the people who use that equipment and work with that technology.

People make the difference. People are at the heart of the changes that have had to take place in organisations in recent years. Working patterns have changed dramatically and there have been major shifts in the way that work is arranged and controlled within organisations.

> **'Our competitors can copy our products, but they can never copy our people!'**
>
> *Managing Director, Manufacturing Company*

Changing to survive

Working patterns in the UK have changed out of all recognition. The era when the majority of the national workforce was employed in simple full-time, long-term jobs has gone for ever. In today's diverse employment environment, only a minority of employment opportunities fit the traditional notion of a 'normal' or 'real' job.

Less than half the UK working population now has a full-time, long-term job with a traditional employment contract; instead there is considerable variety in the way work is organised, as employers pursue greater and greater flexibility.

> **'Work is no longer supplied in neat, seven-and-a-half-hour blocks.'**
>
> *Personnel Director*

Over a quarter of UK jobs are *part time*, of which more than eight out of ten are filled by women. *Job-sharing* is a form of part-time working, in which two people share the same full-time post. *Annual hours* are worked in organisations whose activities are cyclical, where times of attendance are varied to suit the work demand. *Shift-working* has become more widespread and at the same time less standardised, allowing for shifts of varying lengths. *Temporary jobs* are on the increase and *term-time working* is offered by many employers. Employers can even get work done without the need for employment contracts: *franchising, subcontracting and the use of consultants* involve the payment of fees, but there are no direct employment costs.

Whilst these more flexible patterns of working become more prevalent, even greater emphasis is placed on increasing the flexibility of performance when actually at work. Are individuals constrained by narrow, tightly drawn job descriptions or do they use their skills as widely as possible? Showing how jobs can be opened up and the tasks within them made more flexible (and more enjoyable) is one of the aims of this book and there will be more about freeing people to realise their full potential in subsequent chapters.

> **'We must have people who are prepared to be very flexible in their pattern of coming in to work and very versatile when they get here.'**
>
> *Retailing Manager*

In parallel with the shifts in working patterns, organisational structures have also been changing. As companies have responded to competitive pressures and challenges, a number of 'standard' structural forms have emerged.

The pyramid is the oldest structure and is hierarchical, with several levels of management grouped according to technical functions. Managers tend to be experts in their field and simple reward structures support clear career paths.

The flatter structure is designed to have fewer hierarchical levels so as to encourage people within the organisation to play a greater part and to feel that they are valued and have a genuine role. Career paths and reward systems may be less distinct, as the prospects for vertical promotion are substantially reduced. Flatter organisations respond more quickly to customer demands, often through the use of smaller, task-oriented workgroups and by developing sophisticated teamworking. Flatter organisations may also be made *slimmer*, retaining only a small number of permanent staff, with other functions contracted out.

In a *matrix organisation*, there are functional hierarchies to provide the appropriate technical expertise, but the task focus is upon the product, the service or a particular customer group. Multi-disciplinary teams are created to carry out the necessary tasks. The individual reports in two directions: vertically in respect of his or her technical function and horizontally in respect of his or her task group.

In a *project-oriented structure*, people are brought together because they have particular specialist skills or knowledge in order to complete a one-off project. When the individual project objective is achieved, the project group or team is disbanded.

As they develop and grow, organisations can often find that their needs are not met by any single one of the standard structures. As a result, they combine several of these structures in some form, the main criterion for success being that any new structure should support the staff and help them to do their jobs more effectively.

As organisations have experimented with different structures, there is little doubt that the 'flatter' organisation has emerged as a clear winner. The actual structure may vary, the particular needs may be different, but thousands of managers now have to operate in organisations which have 'flattened themselves'. This means fewer layers of management, fewer instances of overlapping decision-making and fewer instances of buck-passing.

> **'We used to be hierarchical, functionally structured and autocratically run. Now we're a customer and process company with a flat structure, where everyone takes responsibility for what they produce.'**
>
> *General Manager, Engineering Company*

Flattening should not be a desperate cost-cutting response to a financial crisis: it should involve controlled change, made during stable economic times. It must be undertaken for positive reasons, which focus upon service to the customer and involve a clear-sighted resolve to eliminate impediments to service, such as rigid hierarchies, unnecessary bureaucracy and a 'not my job' mentality.

As an organisation is flattened, it becomes 'leaner and fitter', so that decision-making becomes more effective. In a traditional hierarchical organisation, decision-making tends to fly ever upward, but the establishment of a more dynamic and flatter organisation ensures that decisions are taken at the point where they need to be made.

The concept of 'inverting' the structure involves placing the company's customers, markets and competitors at the top of the organisational pyramid to emphasise their vital importance. Company employees represent the next layer down, with the management below them. In this way the practical interface between company and customers is emphasised and the role of management in supporting genuine customer service underlined.

Many organisations now find it helpful to represent their structures in the 'upside-down' fashion shown in Figure 1. This helps to reinforce the point that organisational structures should exist to facilitate organisational objectives and not to sustain fantasies of personal status or individual power.

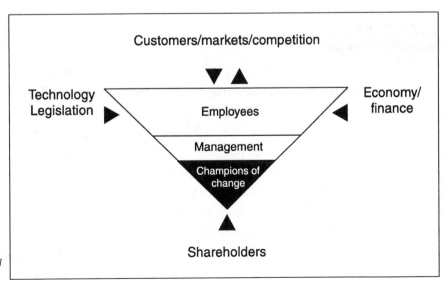

Fig. 1. Inverting the organisational pyramid

The implications of organisational changes

The substantial changes in patterns of employment, coupled with the moves towards less regimented organisational structures, have significant implications both for the management of organisations and for managerial style.

In the last decade, the changing nature of competition, the challenge of global economics, the need to respond quickly to competitive pressures and the widespread availability of information, together with many other challenges, have forced organisations to reassess managerial and leadership styles.

The traditional 'hard-headed' approach, which perpetuated the control of the many by the few, stemmed largely from manufacturing industry. In recent times, however, many more voluntary groups and social organisations have developed, and it is partly from these sources that changes in managerial and leadership styles have sprung.

These voluntary groups and social organisations had to adopt a different approach from that found in traditional manufacturing, because their employees and those people who gave voluntarily of their time did so on an equal basis with 'the management' and recognised that the organisation had values and purposes to which they all subscribed.

Leadership

Organisations have always had leaders, but leadership has never been a static art. Organisational requirements have changed continuously and managerial leadership itself has endeavoured to reflect such shifts, albeit after some procrastination. Thus the leadership skills in an organisation can sometimes lag behind the progress which that same organisation may be making in other respects.

It is important at this point to ask a number of questions. Just what is leadership? How does it manifest itself in managerial situations? Are leaders different from managers? Can a leader be a manager and can a manager be a leader? One way of answering these questions is by looking at the origins of the two particular words.

Managers

The word 'manager' is derived from the Latin *manus*, meaning 'hand'. The sixteenth-century Italian word *maneggiare* comes from this and was applied to the handling, training and control of horses. English soldiers subsequently brought the word back from Italy and applied it to the handling of armies and the control of ships. People who performed these vital jobs became known as 'managers'. Gradually, the word came into more general use and was applied to anyone who had a responsibility for organising activities and controlling their administration.

Leaders

The word 'leader' comes from *laed*, a word common to all the old North European languages, meaning 'path', 'road', 'course of a ship at sea' or 'journey'. A leader therefore accompanies people on a journey, guiding them to their destination. By implication they hold people together as a group whilst leading them in the right direction. A typical modern-day dictionary definition is *one who rules, guides or inspires others*.

The Industrial Society conducted a survey in 1996 which revealed how the two words were viewed. The top six words or phrases which the respondents associated with **managers** were:

- planners
- controllers
- implementers of policy
- resourcers
- administrators
- people who are results-oriented.

For **leaders**, the most commonly associated six words or phrases were as follows:

- motivators
- enablers
- mentors
- communicators
- innovators
- people who are energetic.

The common perception, therefore, is that there is a clear and distinct difference in both the characteristics and the activities of managers and leaders. However, we must beware of concluding that an effective manager cannot also be regarded as an effective leader, or that a charismatic leader will be a poor manager. There is no reason why a given individual should not be equally effective at both leading and managing.

There is evidence to suggest that many very effective managers are not viewed by their staff as leaders, although these self-same managers may well believe that they are good leaders who display leadership. The important phrase in the previous sentence is 'viewed by their staff', which highlights the two-way process which leadership involves. In effect, a leader cannot exercise leadership if those whom he or she aims to lead do not give their consent.

> **'Leadership is a reciprocal relationship between those who choose to lead and those who decide to follow.'**
>
> *James Kouzes and Barry Posner*[1]

The nature of the relationship between a manager and those who are managed is quite different from the relationship between a leader and those who are led.

A management relationship can be perfectly satisfactory if it is brisk and businesslike, with a cool attention paid to tasks and results. Often, there may be an unemotional, job-oriented approach on both sides. A leadership relationship, on the other hand, will not succeed through coolness: there must be warmth, inspiration and a stirring of the blood. A leadership relationship cannot avoid an involvement with the emotions.

The traditional picture of a traditional leader

The traditional image of a great leader is of a strong, charismatic, dynamic and ambitious figure who is dominant, decisive and calculating. It can be argued that this powerful form of self-centred leadership has served us well in the past. Many great companies have

---

[1] *Credibility: How Leaders Gain it and Lose it – Why People Demand it,* James Kouzes and Barry Posner, Jossey-Bass (March 97)

grown and prospered through difficult trading conditions because they had a strong, traditional leader at the helm.

The traditional leader is a 'command and control' leader who demands and gets a staff and a workforce of good soldiers who will do as they are told, obey the rules, ask no questions and face dismissal should they transgress.

Such traditional leadership deliberately builds up dependency and subservience. It does not value the skills and achievements of others and suppresses individual growth and development. By implication, it encourages inefficiency, since the soldiery are not required to think for themselves, and any ideas they may have for improved work practices will not be encouraged. Traditional leadership is associated with the love of power, knowing what is best for others and localising control and privilege within a closed regime.

This image of the traditional leader is a very strong one, stemming as it does from the dictatorial and charismatic leaders who have achieved both fame and notoriety. **There are, however, other kinds of leadership**.

Real organisational leadership

It is a common misconception that leadership is wholly a function of position in a hierarchy. This view implies that 'leadership' resides at the top, whilst 'management' occupies the lower slopes. It is one of the purposes of this book to reject such a view completely and to promote a totally different version of the leadership/management partnership.

> **'Leadership is about getting extraordinary results from ordinary people.'**
>
> *John Harvey Jones[2]*

Leadership as an attribute has nothing to do with a particular position held in some organisational hierarchy. Neither is it a characteristic which is confined to a few forceful, charismatic men and

---

[2] John Harvey-Jones when speaking at an Industrial Society Runge Course (Effective Leadership) in 1992

women. The skills of leadership, and the exercise of leadership, can exist at all levels in an organisation.

If we think about our own lives and careers, we can identify several people whom we would regard as leaders. They are usually people whom we would be prepared to follow, willingly and enthusiastically. Recalling the positions they held, we often realise that few occupied positions of great authority. We regarded them as leaders and followed them because of their leadership skills, not because of any particular position they held. Nor did we follow them because they were powerful or had control over us. Rather, we regarded them as worth following for what they said and did.

Similarly, those working in the large 'middle ground' of an organisation will just as readily focus upon a colleague at the same hierarchical level as upon someone in a management position. Indeed, experienced managers will often follow the lead of a more junior person. In a productive working environment leaders are not commanders, controllers, bosses or big shots; they are servants, supporters, partners and providers.

Leadership is a set of highly tuned skills, behaviours and practices that can be learned regardless of whether or not one is in a formal management position.

The competitive advantage which every organisation seeks may be achieved through quality, price, customer care, product innovation, delivery time or after-sales service. All these practical aspects are within the direct control of an organisation's staff and workforce. The challenge for leaders and managers is to create a climate which allows people to look for and achieve continual improvements in competitiveness.

It is the function of an organisation's leadership to recognise that its people are the key to competitive advantage and to stimulate, inspire and encourage them to achieve that advantage. That is what is meant by leading effectively.

As organisations change, leadership must change

People in today's workforce have today's expectations, which requires a different kind of leadership system: one which does not consist of a single thinking leader and a large group of unthinking followers, but demands shared thinking and leadership. The days of the strong, self-willed, domineering leader are over. Such leaders are being replaced by people who are more in tune with today's economic and social climate.

> **'We don't direct people any more, we direct the traffic – make sure it's running smoothly.'**
>
> *Chief Executive, Manufacturing Company*

Today, all those former 'good soldiers' who would unquestioningly do exactly as they were told (even though they often knew better ways of working and achieving results) are no longer available. People will not subscribe to that kind of submissiveness nowadays.

Progressive companies have recognised that it impossible for them to compete merely by using the brains and constructive energy of a few senior people for decision-making. Modern complexities mean that the burdens placed upon the few are too great. In order to survive and prosper in today's competitive market, an organisation must utilise all the expertise and energy at its disposal.

> **'Leadership denotes unleashing energy, building, freeing and growing.'**
>
> *Tom Peters*[3]

Today's competitive environment requires an organisational culture in which all the energies of all the employees are focused upon the customer. Effective leadership creates a climate which harnesses all the brainpower of all the people.

Leadership for today – and for tomorrow

Research studies and surveys conducted by The Industrial Society have helped to identify the leadership characteristics required today, tomorrow and forward into the twenty-first century. One of these

---

[3] *Passion for Excellence,* Tom Peters and Nancy Austin, Fontana (August 96)

studies involved an extensive literature review and the development of a questionnaire, which was then completed by a representative sample of respondents working for a wide range of organisations.

The questionnaire asked people to indicate how they defined and identified leadership behaviour, homing in upon the leadership experienced by individuals in their domestic, social and work lives. Partly as a result of casting the net so widely, not all the examples of leadership given in the responses concerned leaders who were in designated positions of authority. Such a diversity of settings was deliberately sought, as it enabled the Society to establish a view of leadership which covers both the organisational and the social.

When the questionnaires were analysed, a picture emerged of the kind of leadership to which people respond and the type of leader who can command respect. Leaders were described as those who helped others through a sticky patch, lightened their burden, enhanced their appreciation of an event by relieving them of associated administrative tasks or provided support or direction. Underlying many of the anecdotes was the theme of leader honesty and integrity, and the assumption that their acts of leadership were not carried out for personal gain. The leaders described by the respondents displayed strong beliefs both in themselves and in others and exhibited demonstrable competencies, the effect of which was evidenced by their impact on others. Here is a selection of the examples of leadership behaviour cited by the respondents:

> 'Consistent, good, strong leadership through leading meetings, structure of pastoral system, individual relationships, clear vision and yet humility and self-sacrifice.'

> 'Leading by example and providing guidance and coaching over an extended period.'

> 'A consistently good leader who listened well, coaxed ideas out of people, helped to formulate them and credited the originators with them.'

> 'My boss consistently managed my group by using a strong blend of ambition, enthusiasm, friendliness and fairness.'

'Took time to listen to people and took an interest in the day-to-day problems and ambitions of employees. His technical judgement was excellent, but he respected other people's knowledge and areas of expertise also. Always did his best for people.'

'Great at encouraging and delegating. Gets the best out of people. Gets people to develop and uncovers untapped talents. Excellent judge of people.'

'Communicated a coherent set of goals. Made judgements based on evidence. Matched empowerment with responsibility.'

'Clear thinking, good communicator, real vision, ethical with values, high standards, honest and open.'

'Did not interfere with day-to-day routine work. Quite "laid back" but very knowledgeable and inspired respect. Prepared to back her staff in disputes with clients. Was not a careerist only out for herself.'

In addition to managers in organisations many different people were identified as leaders by the sample population. Amongst those listed were friends, teachers, priests, archaeologists, social workers, captains of sports teams, colleagues at work, parents, course leaders, holiday representatives, management consultants, scout leaders and members of the public.

The responses to the questionnaire indicated that the benefits accruing from good leadership were many. There were instances when the style of leadership enabled people to give of their best. At other times, by taking the lead, the leader voluntarily accepted the burden of organisation and management of a group or situation with the approval of those being led.

Creating a climate for success was seen as good leadership, as was the ability of leaders to elicit improved performance from those who reported to them. There were cases where the appropriate display of good leadership in taking balanced judgements had removed inherent conflict. Some leaders were so acknowledged purely because they were willing to admit their errors, thus freeing those they led to correct a wayward course created by misjudgement. Others were judged to be good leaders because they were able to bring warring factions together and minimise the fallout from a difficult situation. Liberating people to make considered decisions by keeping them informed was also seen as good leadership.

> **'Winning companies are led by visionary and enthusiastic champions of change.'**
>
> *Department of Trade and Industry*

It is clear that this good leadership behaviour has both a 'visible' and an 'invisible' component. The visible component is represented by the competencies displayed, but the invisible component is derived from the *belief system* of the leader.

The belief system of a leader can best be defined as the underlying assumptions which the leader makes when leading or dealing with others. Research has identified the following three main beliefs:

1. *Self-belief:* The inner assurance of the individual and the conviction that he or she can take on and triumph over the situation they are facing. They remain unruffled under pressure and take charge in a crisis.

2. *Belief in, and beliefs about, others*: Being sensitive to the needs and moods of other people and being true to their underlying beliefs about others. Seeing good in others and not exploiting those who depend on them.

3. *Belief in fairness*: Being even-handed in their dealing with people and leaving others feeling that they have been fairly treated. This usually comes from making judgements only after hearing all the facts and admitting to fallibility, ignorance and similar frailties.

These beliefs are manifested in the way that leaders apply their skills and competencies. For example, when real leaders communicate, according to the survey respondents, they speak with inner conviction, their communications are sensitive to the feelings and expectations of others and they are regarded as fair to all those reading their words or listening to them. In contrast, people who might occupy leadership positions but who are not regarded as real leaders will mouth the platitudes of their manager, be self-oriented and subjective in what they say, communicating in ways designed to make a favourable impression on their superiors.

The research has shown that the beliefs of leaders and potential leaders are of paramount importance, impacting upon what they do and the way that they do it. Since, however, it is their actions and not their thoughts that are observed by others, we should perhaps reverse the previous sentence to read: *what they do and the way that they do it reflects what they believe.*

In everyday organisational management, personal beliefs can come into play in many different situations. The organisation may have systems and procedures and the manager may have a job description, but that manager's beliefs can still affect the way in which the task is performed:

- If the manager does not believe in the importance of **open communication**, then he or she may be secretive and fail to share information with his or her staff. Whilst some information may be transmitted the general approach will demonstrate a lack of enthusiasm for communication.
- If the manager does not believe in the importance of **briefing** others, then he or she may not prepare thoroughly for briefing sessions and may not run them effectively. Even though a system is in place, and others are committed to it, the lack of belief can result in a manager going through the motions and achieving very little.
- If the manager does not believe in the importance of **staff appraisal**, then he or she may not prepare properly for appraisal sessions and may not carry them out effectively. There may be well-established procedures and other people may operate them enthusiastically, but if that one manager is an unbeliever, the company scheme will be weakened.
- In a similar way, if the manager does not believe in **teamwork**, then he or she may not build a team effectively. As in other cases, the motions may be gone through, but the result will not be acceptable.

- By the same token, if a manager does not **trust** people, then other people are unlikely to trust him or her. This is a particularly insidious situation, because lack of trust can quickly destroy relationships and undermine organisational stability. Trustworthiness is a significant discriminant between the true leaders who are followed and those in leadership positions who must be obeyed because of their hierarchical status rather than their leadership.

This recent work has shown that beliefs play a crucial part in determining performance and behaviour and that this element is considerably more important than was previously realised. Much greater attention must be paid to this aspect in order to select and develop better managerial leaders for the future.

The leadership required in the twenty-first century

This comprehensive databank of information, views and opinions gathered from a wide range of research studies and practical experience provides compelling evidence of the need for a new kind of leadership. This leadership should be:

- diffused through an organisation, not concentrated at the top
- shared democratically, rather than placed in the hands of a small élite
- able to lead by living example, instead of through impersonal edict
- capable of providing and sharing a clear vision and direction
- rooted in high ethical standards and shared values
- willing to empower others and give them genuine responsibility
- constantly encouraging, stimulating and supporting others
- always positive, always building and always developing
- based on a belief in the good in people and its enhancement
- friendly, honest, open and fair
- ready to communicate, communicate, communicate!

CHAPTER 2

Liberating leadership: a new style for a new century

Today's leadership requirements

Empowering

Organisations need to replace any remnants of the old-style 'top-down' leadership with a democratically diffused leadership which harnesses the capabilities of all for maximum effectiveness. Those who perform the actual component tasks of work – designing, producing, dealing with customers, delivering products and services – must be allowed to contribute collective leadership to the organisation as a whole.

Empowering is a vogue word which is taken to mean giving individuals personal responsibility for improving the way they do their jobs and strengthening their contribution to the organisation's goals. Regrettably, however, empowering has become associated with job reductions, badly managed change, increases in individual workload and double standards. The cloud which hangs over the word is disturbing, because true empowerment should be the key which unlocks the latent talents and resources of an organisation, making it more responsive, competitive and cost-effective.

'Actually, you can't empower people: you can only create a climate in which they can empower themselves.'

Managing Director, Engineering Company

Liberating

The Industrial Society has adopted the term *liberating* to describe the process of unlocking the skills and capabilities of all the people in an organisation by giving them real responsibility and accountability. Whilst empowering suggests the giving of some power, with an implicit threat that the power could be withdrawn, liberating involves the concept of drawing out and utilising the abilities, strengths and flair of individuals.

Liberating requires a fundamental shift in attitude and belief and an organisation-wide campaign to change the behaviour of both managers and front-line staff. Liberating puts into practice the belief that to be successful, organisations must harness the creativity and brainpower of all their employees, rather than that of just a few managers.

'I think everyone has something to give. It's my job to find out what that is and then make it count.'

Production Manager

To be successful, liberating programmes must have the backing of everyone and the organisation's senior team should demonstrate their total commitment by their day-to-day behaviour. Liberating must apply to the entire organisation, and all managers must be given the freedom that liberating demands.

Liberating is, however, a gradual process, often taking several years. It cannot be achieved by instant decree. The transfer of ownership, and the pushing back of the boundaries of the job, should be systematically planned and people prepared for their new responsibilities. There must be absolute clarity of accountability during the transition.

'We used to have a staff who just worked here: now we have a staff who feel they belong here. They *are* the company.'

Managing Director

Liberating leadership

Creating the right environment

Liberating leadership creates an environment of trust, in which managers exist to support the front-line staff rather than to check on them. Mistakes are viewed as learning opportunities and people feel able to express their views and point out problems, without fear of retribution.

'I see myself as providing a service, rather than exercising control.'

Managing Director

The values of the business at all levels must be defined and translated into behaviours. Managers must live those values and be seen to live them. Senior people must be clear about their vision for business success through liberating leadership, and articulate it clearly and widely at all levels.

The role of managers throughout the organisation must inevitably change from the simpler one of control to a much more subtle position which supports, coaches, provides direction and offers resources. Clearly, managerial job-holders should be given the coaching, help and support to make such a change. The liberating leader's success should be measured by the effective growth of their people.

'Our managers used to be terrified of the idea that the people on the shopfloor know more about the job than they do. Of course they do! That's how it ought to be! A manager's job is to coach, to facilitate and to lead, so that people know their jobs even better.'

Production Director

Structures

Traditional vertical hierarchies build barriers between departments. People are rewarded for 'fighting their own corner', rather than acting in the interests of the business as a whole. These barriers can lead to indifferent customer service – the customer usually experiences the business 'horizontally'.

By flattening the structure and organising around key processes, rather than particular tasks or functions, employees can concentrate on satisfying customers instead of the managerial hierarchy. This can often lead to the introduction of multi-skilled or multi-functional teams. Whilst flatter structures may provide fewer traditional promotion opportunities, horizontal 'promotions' and involvement in projects can present fresh challenges to those who would otherwise become 'plateaued'.

> **'We removed a lot of barriers and reorganised the company into logical, manageable chunks.'**
>
> *Managing Director*

Individuals

Individuals will accept the opportunities that liberation presents, particularly if they feel unfulfilled in their current role. They need to understand the liberating initiative, however, and just what is involved in accepting ownership of their jobs. They must also be given the opportunity (and encouragement) to increase their skills and keep abreast of the needs of their developing role.

The only way to overcome natural reluctance, fear and misunderstanding amongst individuals is through planned training, development and coaching. Whilst a liberating climate presents opportunities for self-development, which can result in a more capable person, not only at work but also outside the working environment, this will not happen overnight.

Liberated teams

Effective leaders have for many years recognised the importance of teamwork. Liberated people will achieve more when they are a part of a team than they would as individuals. The cliché that 'a team is greater than the sum of its parts' can be true but will be realised only when the team has a clear direction and goals. Teamwork should operate everywhere, not just on the front line.

'We want our people to be masters of their own destiny.'

Company Chairman

Much has been achieved with self-managed work teams, where many of the tasks previously done by managers and supervisors are carried out by team members. Scheduling, liaising with other departments and the recruitment of new team members are three examples of such tasks.

Where teams have a permanent leader who works alongside the rest of the team, that person's role is one of coach, facilitator and role model. The leader's role will change as the team matures and members become more able to accept responsibility. Where there is no permanent leader, direction, guidance and challenge must be provided from outside the confines of the immediate team. Every team needs a coach, irrespective of its level of seniority or experience, to help eliminate any barriers to team success, whether real or perceived.

'Nowadays, our teams start pushing the leader, not the other way about.'

Team Leader, Engineering Company

The liberating leader

What is a practising liberating leader like? How does he or she behave? Will the introduction of liberating leaders send shock waves through your organisation? Will it be the end of civilisation as you know it? No – liberating leaders are just people who subscribe to the principles of liberating leadership and therefore practise them.

> **'The role of anyone in leadership is to encourage and advise.'**
>
> *Managing Director*

The liberating leader earns the respect of others by setting a good example. Doing so will not automatically ensure that everyone else follows, but it does contribute to the liberating environment. Liberating leaders who require, set and agree standards for others are obligated to adhere to those standards themselves. They have to 'walk the talk' and show by their own behaviour that they are fully integrated with the organisation, not separated from it.

> **'I believe in management by walking about: I'm a resource for people to use.'**
>
> *Chief Executive*

Surveys have shown that those being led regard enthusiasm as the most important attribute in a leader, and it follows that the liberating leader should be a confirmed enthusiast. Enthusiasm infects people and becomes an effective motivator. The enthusiastic attitude of a genuinely liberating leader encourages to a spirit of 'can do', where problems are seen as challenges to overcome rather than blocks on progress.

As well as enthusiasm, the liberating leader needs a cool head in the midst of a crisis. If other team members tend to panic when the pressure is on, a leader must exert a calming influence.

Liberating leaders must to some extent represent the organisation to others in their team. The leader is both a part of the team and a link to the 'wider team'. The liberating leader must understand and explain the actions of the organisation in a positive way, even when corporate direction appears to contradict local or team requirements.

Knocking the organisation, either directly or by inference, can only have a negative effect and liberating leaders should never, never do it. They must be seen to believe in the organisation and the direction in which it is heading, publicly guiding their teams towards these corporate goals and visions. In addition, liberating leaders demonstrate that the local and team goals and visions are compatible with those of the organisation as a whole.

The essence of a liberating environment is that people feel valued, respected and appreciated – and therefore free to contribute as fully as possible to the organisation. These feelings are generated by their contacts and dealings with colleagues and leaders. Liberating leaders are constantly under observation when dealing with people and they must not be found wanting. They must believe in and appreciate others and they should treat everyone with suitable respect and dignity.

'Everyone is equally valued as a member of the team.'

Chief Executive, National Charity

Liberating leaders apply effective self-management to their own behaviour and must be seen to do so. All standards of conduct, such as timekeeping and attendance, must be rigidly applied to themselves. Standards of performance, work rate and application must also be highly visible to all. Successful liberating leaders have to be seen to be well organised and efficient, exhibiting good time management and effective prioritisation, so that others are encouraged to follow the same path. They should always appear to be 'on top of the job' and avoid anything which smacks of crisis management.

Effective liberating leaders must always show that they are developing themselves on a continuous basis. The concept of the 'learning organisation' is essential to a liberating environment, and it must be demonstrated, not just merely encouraged. The genuine liberating leader will continue to absorb new knowledge and improve key skills, sharing them with the team as appropriate.

'I'm still learning. I travel around a lot and I always look for any little nuggets I can take back and use.'

Managing Director, Toiletries

The physical appearance of a liberating leader is important. Certain situations, such as customer contact and commercial environments, demand a specific image and dress code. The liberating leader should not be misled into thinking that an open and liberating atmosphere means that a sloppy personal appearance is of no consequence. A fresh, alert and fit demeanour have much more impact than a tired, slovenly and careless presence. Leaders who appear stressed and seem to carry the troubles of the world on their shoulders are very unlikely to motivate others in any meaningful way.

Becoming a liberating leader

We've looked at the changing face of leadership and shown that a liberating climate created by a liberating leadership is essential for the future. So what's in it for you? Where do you stand? Do you want to become a liberating leader and, if so, how do you set about becoming one?

At this point your response might be: 'This is all very interesting, but it isn't really for me, thank you very much. I don't like a lot of upset and change, so I think I'll just wait and see for a while. In any case, it isn't me you should be asking – it's them!'

Many people resist change automatically and sometimes almost unthinkingly. It is natural for an individual to feel that change should start not with him or her, but elsewhere. They may accept that their organisation has many problems, but feel very strongly that remedying those problems is a matter for someone else. Top management – they're the ones who ought to change, if anyone should.

Such 'us and them' feelings are understandable, particularly if the individual concerned has been brought up under a strict leadership regime. The introduction of any new and different managerial approach must be instigated by 'the top' and, as change is implemented, it should begin at 'the top'. Any attempt to make sweeping changes in managerial practices at the middle and lower levels, whilst maintaining the *status quo* at the top, will not succeed.

The introduction of liberating leadership into an organisation cannot be carried out in that way. Since one of the objectives is to create a liberating climate that is open, democratic, conflict-free and flexible, the introductory process itself must reflect such features. Liberation cannot be forced through by diktat!

It follows that the best way for an organisation to move to a liberating climate is by consent. Everyone in the organisation needs to learn what liberating leadership is and then want to experience it. It can be introduced gradually, as people embrace the principles and start to put them into practice.

> **'You cannot be a quality company unless you believe in your staff and invest in them.'**
>
> *General Manager, Electrical Goods*

Liberating leadership is not another half-baked organisational concept, to be seized upon by a desperate Board of Directors, introduced in haste with inadequate preparation, misunderstood by the majority and then left to briefly flower and fade before the recriminations set in. Liberating leadership will not exist at all unless it is introduced properly.

You can make a start now

The concept of 'leadership' in liberating leadership is a new one. It is leadership which is not confined to the top, but spread widely and diffused downwards through the organisation as a whole. Thus, it follows that everyone must learn about it and feel comfortable with it. So, although you might believe instinctively that other people should start learning first, that would be a mistake. Now is the time for you to step forward, now is the time for you to stand up and be counted. Liberating leadership is sound, attractive and worthwhile and you ought to be in on it from the beginning.

Indeed, you don't have to wait. Even though your own organisation may not adopt liberating leadership just yet, even though your own chief executive has still to be persuaded, even though there are so many obstacles, the sooner you start learning about it the better.

As soon as you become familiar with liberating leadership and understand it, you can start implementing some of its principles in your everyday routine. You can make a start without having to wait for your bosses to set up a fully fledged system.

Of course what you can do depends upon your current managerial position and responsibilities. You might be able to effect a marked shift in approach and emphasis immediately, or you may have to content yourself with minor innovations until other people who are organisationally linked with you have undergone a learning process and can catch up.

> **'I want my managers to interact with their people in exactly the same way that I interact with them.'**
>
> *Managing Director, Gas Turbine Manufacturer*

Gradually, however, you will be able to do more and have a greater impact. As you put further aspects of liberating leadership into place, you will reap the benefits. You will be in a very strong position when your organisation finally adopts liberating leadership and makes a concerted effort to implement it across the company. So start now and get ahead of the game! Your hour will come!

The Industrial Society can help you with the learning process, through its range of special courses in liberating leadership, tailored specifically for different managerial groups in organisations. You can help yourself by using this book, which sets out the principles and practices of liberating leadership for you to study, either on its own or as a companion to the courses. And you can help yourself further by implementing those principles and practices in your present workplace, so that you can learn through practical experience. If you can persuade a colleague to learn with you, sharing each other's experiences, so much the better.

> **'We have to keep on getting better. No one should be satisfied with the *status quo*.'**
>
> *HR Manager, Pharmaceuticals*

If you can pioneer liberating leadership, you will be in a strong position to make a real contribution to the vigour and competitiveness of your organisation. Share the concept with others by using a simple slogan, devised by The Industrial Society, which conveys the flavour of liberating leadership.

LEADER

Our slogan is easy to remember: it consists of only six letters, which spell out the word LEADER.

The concept of liberating leadership is encapsulated in six themic activities which can be memorised by means of a useful mnemonic. Since, however, the perfectly proper and correct word 'mnemonic' (*aiding or intended to aid one's memory*) always looks like a typing error, in this book we shall use the word 'slogan'!

Use the slogan LEADER to help you to summarise how liberating leadership constructs a basis for achieving results in today's competitive business world. The message of the slogan is that in order for staff to regard their managers as liberating leaders those managers need to practise all six activities listed in Figure 2.

	LIBERATE	by freeing those closest to the job to take their own decisions
	ENCOURAGE	their staff and support them where necessary
	ACHIEVE	the purpose for which the team, department or organisation exists
	DEVELOP	people and teams
Set an	**E**XAMPLE	by their own behaviour
Build	**R**ELATIONSHIPS	based on trust

Fig. 2. The Liberating Leader slogan

A liberating leadership profile

If you are to turn yourself into a liberating leader, what sort of practical activities will you have to engage in on a day-to-day basis?

'Lots of people can have good ideas, but that's not leadership. A real leader can turn those ideas into action, by inspiring and motivating people and getting the very best out of them.'

Managing Director

To help you to establish the required range of practical activities, actions and behaviours, a profiling instrument has been developed by The Industrial Society for use with the liberating leadership concept. It consists of a bank of thirty-eight statements which have to be rated for their degree of applicability to a given individual. The statements are examples of what a leader does on a regular basis.

The subject carries out a self-rating test, examining each statement of behaviour (for example, *consults those affected before making decisions*) and grading it according to how closely it matches his or her daily behaviour at work. In addition, the same profiling instrument is issued to others who work with the subject (colleagues, and people for whom the subject is responsible) and their profiles are then made available for comparison. Conclusions may be drawn from the relationship between an individual's self-assessed profile and those drawn up by informed observers.

Following the development of the slogan LEADER, the thirty-eight behavioural statements were grouped according to the six themic activities. The result is a Behaviour Profile of the ideal liberating leader:

THE LEADER PROFILE

Liberates
- Does not blame people for mistakes
- Encourages the people closest to the job to take their own decisions
- Listens to their staff
- Encourages full and open communication
- Operates systems based on trust, rather than suspicion
- Encourages staff to develop new ideas

Encourages and supports
- Accepts responsibility for the actions of their staff
- Gives praise where it is due
- Recognises, and acts to minimise, other people's stress
- Supports staff when they need support
- Regularly meets with individuals to clarify direction
- Makes people feel important and shows that they have faith in them

Achieves purpose
- Achieves results
- Agrees demanding targets with individuals or teams
- Consults those affected before making decisions
- Is willing to take unpopular decisions in order to move forward
- Seeks out future challenges/opportunities
- Regularly communicates an inspirational view of the future
- Constantly seeks to improve the way things are done

Develops people and teams
- Encourages other people to learn
- Encourages people to work together as a team
- Regularly meets with the team, as a whole, to review progress
- Takes time to develop and guide their staff
- Deals effectively with breaches in standards of behaviour
- Treats other people's mistakes as learning opportunities

Example to others
- Actively encourages feedback on their own performance
- Communicates an air of enthusiasm
- Works on their own learning
- Practises what they preach
- Openly admits mistakes
- Sets a good example to others by their own behaviour

Relationships built on trust
- Does not put self-interest before interests of their staff
- Keeps promises and does what they say they will do
- Is in touch with, and sensitive to, people's feelings
- Is calm in a crisis, and when under pressure
- Is honest and truthful
- Does not take personal credit for other people's work
- Is always fair

The LEADER Pie

The Behaviour Profile is used regularly in surveys and by individuals to identify current strengths and areas for future development.

Respondents have also been asked to indicate the importance that they attach to each of the thirty-eight behavioural statements. It is of considerable interest to reveal the results from this aspect of the feedback. The 'pie' in Figure 3 shows the importance, by category, of the six groups of behaviours.

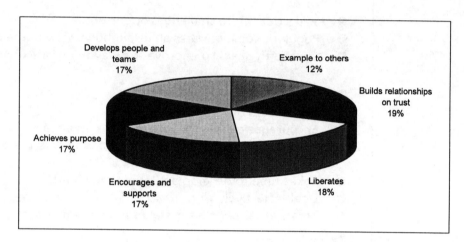

Fig. 3.
LEADER:
importance by
category

Whilst the six are distributed in a fairly even fashion, it is worth remarking that the greatest importance is given to 'Builds Relationships on Trust', reinforcing the earlier point that it is the beliefs of the liberating leader and the way they manifest themselves as actions that is the key to leadership achievement.

The good leadership equation

It is what people actually do that enables others to recognise good leadership. The survey undertaken by The Industrial Society, and subsequent analysis of its results, has enabled the following equation to be formulated to delineate good leadership:

| **recognition of leadership** | = | **leadership skills and practices** | + | **aligned beliefs** | + | **trusting relationships** |

This equation indicates that people will recognise real leadership if they can identify the presence of all three different groups of attributes in an individual. There must be a clear demonstration of leadership skills and practices, accompanied by evidence of aligned beliefs and the establishment of a trusting relationship.

The Liberating Leader Ship

Building on the good leadership equation, The Industrial Society has developed an illustrative analogy which takes the form of a sailing vessel – The Liberating Leader Ship.

The results of the survey conducted by the Society indicated that there were two broad areas which gave rise to the recognition of leadership:

1. Behaviours which are leadership skills, competencies and practices.
2. Behaviours which build trust.

Behaviours in the first category are easy to recognise. Managers and leaders display them on a daily basis: when setting targets, conducting team meetings and in coaching their staff. It would only take an hour or so to ascertain whether a new leader possessed a recognisable range of leadership skills, competencies and practices.

Behaviours in the second category are not so obvious. They become evident gradually as people draw conclusions from what they see and hear. A person might conclude, for example, that their leader is basically fair or that they do not put their personal interests above those of their staff. These conclusions will take some time to reach, because they depend upon the observation of certain small clues and pointers. These second category behaviours are thus more submerged.

Both categories of behaviour spring from basic beliefs. Underlying assumptions influence both the leadership skills, competencies and practices and the behaviours which build up the trust of others and create sound relationships. We can refer to these beliefs as *aligned beliefs*, because they line up with and give rise to the behaviours.

The Liberating Leader Ship analogy allows us to present the two sorts of behaviour together with the aligned beliefs as a sailing ship which is underway (see Figure 4 overleaf). There are three principal features of this vessel which can be used and labelled:

1. The *hull* above the water line must be sound and strong: it represents the *leadership skills, competencies and practices*.

2.   The *hull* below the water line must be resilient and unyielding: it represents the *aligned beliefs of the leader.*
3.   The *keel* is essential to any voyage: it represents the *relationship of trust which the leader must engender.*

To undertake any successful voyage, both the upper and lower hull and the keel must be sound and well built. They must also be in balance: the size of the keel must be appropriate to the size of the hull. As with all such models and analogies in the human resources area, we must not be too fanciful or push comparisons too far. The Liberating Leader Ship is, however, a useful illustration of the following guideline:

> **Anyone in a managerial role who wants to be regarded as an effective leader and to gain the commitment and support of their staff must not only possess a full portfolio of leadership skills and practices but must also win the trust of the people concerned. They can, however, only demonstrate those skills and achieve that trust if their underlying beliefs (self-belief, belief in, and beliefs about, others, and belief in fairness) are strong enough to sustain the behavioural consistency which leadership demands.**

Fig. 4. The Liberating Leader Ship

Six letters – six chapters

Each of the six letters of your slogan LEADER represents a segment of the portfolio of activities, actions and behaviour that you need to arm yourself with in order to be an effective liberating leader. In the six chapters which follow, we take you through each letter and thus each segment in turn. In each chapter we look at what you, the potential liberating leader, need to do to match the actions which that particular segment requires, examining two of the specialised skills which you will require and giving you some advice to help you brush up on them, together with a useful checklist of actions.

It should be noted that these 'skill' sections do not cover the topics concerned with the depth and thoroughness contained in the multiplicity of books, articles, videos, audiotapes, CD-ROMs and computer-based learning products which are available to purchase, borrow or hire. Our tips and checklists, however, are designed to show how each particular skill or area of expertise relates to liberating leadership.

CHAPTER 3

L means 'liberates'

Our slogan LEADER begins with 'L' for LIBERATES. So the first characteristic of the liberating leader (and this is as it should be) is that he or she *liberates* others.

If a manager or a leader or a manager-leader liberates other people, those people have greater personal ownership and demonstrate greater responsibility for the aspects of their work they can influence and which they experience as 'theirs'. Liberating people frees them from the shackles of the traditional command and control structure, which can stifle initiative, foster subservience and lead to the growth of inefficiency.

Liberating managers and leaders need to encourage those people who are nearest to the tasks to feel a sense of ownership by giving them the authority, responsibility and resources to take the decisions which they are competent to take. People will accept additional responsibility if they are given the necessary information and training and if they know that they won't be blamed for any mistakes. As already mentioned, the transfer of ownership and any pushing back of the boundaries of the job should be systematically planned and people prepared for their new responsibilities. There must be clarity of accountability during any such transitional period.

The profile of 'liberates'

If YOU are going to become a liberating leader, then you need to make sure that you can LIBERATE. This means, as the LEADER Profile indicates:

- not blaming your staff for their mistakes
- encouraging the people closest to the job to take their own decisions
- listening to your staff
- encouraging full and open communication
- operating systems based on trust, not suspicion
- encouraging your staff to develop new ideas.

You need to look at each of these in more detail, although you must remember that they are not necessarily separate and distinct aspects of behaviour. Rather, they represent a 'portfolio' of behaviours which you, when you become a liberating leader, will display. The components of this portfolio are usually interlinked, so that if you show an inclination towards liberating behaviour in one element of the portfolio, you would be expected to show it in all of them.

Conversely, it would be very unlikely, for example, for you to encourage the people closest to the job to take their own decisions and encourage staff to develop new ideas, whilst at the same time blaming people for mistakes and voicing suspicions about their actions. This would represent uncharacteristic behaviour, whereas the behaviours of the liberating leader are always very much in character, displaying a consistency, harmony and a sense of reinforcement. It is such consistency that you must seek to emulate.

For that reason the various behaviours which we have identified cannot usually be learned and developed individually. Rather, they are part of a general climate of liberation which fits together. Nevertheless, it is simpler for you to think about them one by one initially.

Not blaming your staff for their mistakes
You will seek acknowledgement from the other person that a mistake has been made, discuss the nature of the mistake and how it came to

happen, work out with the other person how things could have been done differently and agree to use the incident as a learning experience. You should do this on a one-to-one basis and not make public reference to the mistake.

Managers with less democratic styles have been known to blame mistakes on individuals who were not in fact responsible. This kind of injustice stems from a managerial approach which sees people in the mass rather than as individuals. It can occur when people and their skills are not valued and little or no consideration is given to the self-esteem of individuals.

> **'If someone makes a mistake, we don't waste time blaming them for it – we find out why they made it.'**
>
> *Production Manager*

You, as a liberating leader, will have more appreciation of the qualities and skills of others and will recognise how important it is to regard everyone as an individual and to treat them accordingly. When errors are made, you will not approach such instances in a cavalier fashion: proper enquiry will be made and each mistake used as a stepping-stone for the person concerned.

Encouraging the people closest to the job to take their own decisions
You will value the fact that people close to the job know a great deal about it and are therefore capable of making and taking effective decisions. You must ensure that they have the necessary training and information to allow this to happen. Older leadership styles tended to hold on to the levers of decision-making, but this could often create a dependency culture and the attitude given expression in the corny old cliché: 'it's more than my job's worth, squire!'

Listening to your staff
Listening is a greatly neglected skill and leaders who instinctively close their ears can find that other people start to do the same to them. You will always listen actively and welcome feedback. You need to listen

carefully in order to understand the other person's views before you venture a response. Don't just regard listening as the pauses between your own speeches: if someone wants to air an issue with you, however repetitively, you must hear them out.

'After a bit of a struggle, we've got our people listening actively now, not passively.'

HR Manager

Encouraging full and open communication

As a liberating leader, you will not keep your staff in the dark. You will recognise that full and open communication ensures that accurate information flows freely to people who can benefit from it. As a result, your staff will know what is going on and feel part of the corporate family, carrying out their duties with enhanced commitment.

Leaders who use a more traditional style are often less interested in communication with their staff. If there are any remnants of the old attitude of 'the less they know the better', important information may not be passed on. Some managers feel that information is power and are resolved to maintain that power in their own hands.

'If you're going to delegate, you must communicate!'

HR Manager

Operating systems based on trust, not suspicion

It has been shown that trust is one of the major components of the liberating leadership style. There are many, many behaviours which destroy trust. Amongst these are:

- inconsistency
- not being supportive
- taking the credit for a team result or for another person's success
- appearing to have a 'do as I say, not as I do' attitude
- being reluctant to make commitments or promises
- failing to keep any promises made
- moving the goalposts

- taking decisions without consultation
- failing to communicate
- criticising people in public
- refusing to accept responsibility.

You, by contrast, as a liberating leader, will be active in building up trust. You will do this through your honesty and openness, by communicating freely, by admitting your mistakes, by being consistent and, above all, by delivering your promises. You should not impose systems or procedures that imply suspicion, such as clocking in, the countersigning of vouchers or a regime of 'reporting in'. If people feel that they are under surveillance, trust will be destroyed.

Encouraging your staff to develop new ideas
You will recognise that people who are doing a particular job and have lengthy experience of it can often be a source of very useful ideas. Some leaders often feel that their staff should not be involved in the generation of ideas, but you will value any contribution which they make to the development of new concepts across the company.

New ideas which apply to a relatively small compass of work are often just as useful as ideas which aspire to become the grand corporate scheme for the future. If you can encourage such small proposals and help to get them adopted, it will show people that their ideas are valued and stimulate them to put forward others.

> **'He's always coming up with ideas – but when someone brings him a better one, he's absolutely delighted: he dumps his own idea and goes with the other one.'**
>
> *PA to Managing Director*

Your attributes, skills and competencies

The six behaviours which characterise L FOR LIBERATES are underpinned by particular attributes, skills or competencies which you, as a liberating leader, will need to use. We close this chapter by featuring two of these, which you may need to extend or develop: **listening skills** and the **promotion of innovation**.

Listening: tips for liberating leaders

Listening is both one of the most important interpersonal skills and the hardest to master. There are two varieties – passive and active. Passive listening is a way of 'listening but not really listening', where people appear to be paying attention to what is being said to them, but are simply letting the words pass them by. You, as a liberating leader, must be able to achieve active listening at all times – that is, you must concentrate hard and absorb the content and meaning of what is being said to you.

In conversation, you should not only listen to what the other person is saying but also try to formulate a reply. You must be in control of this process of listening, thinking and interpolating a response, so that your understanding of the content of the conversation is not impaired. Unless you really understand what the other person is trying to say, you cannot very easily interpret their meaning. Furthermore, unless you can convey during the conversation that you are truly listening, the other person will not be confident that you are giving them a fair and proper hearing.

More effective listening

To make your listening more effective, you need to be aware of several vital practical aspects and to practise these until you become conversant with them.

Learn to *concentrate* effectively on what the other person is saying. It requires hard work and practice to clear your mind of all your own thoughts and to focus exclusively on the other person for an appropriate length of time.

Practise *following a train of thought* – it is not enough just to listen to the words being spoken.

Learn to tune into *feelings and emotions* so that you can understand the other person better. Listen to 'the music behind the words' and try to imagine how the other person really feels.

Learn to curb your natural instincts and *let them talk*. By keeping quiet and allowing the other person to do most of the talking, you will glean much more.

Summarise from time to time and get them to agree with your summary, to check your understanding and demonstrate to them that you really are listening.

Learn to *clarify* the information being received. You should probe gently and quietly at natural points in the conversation, without cutting across them or interrupting.

Use *eye contact* to encourage the other person and to show them that they have your undivided attention. Don't stare at them all the time: allow your gaze to shift gently away from them and back again in a natural way.

Give *non-verbal prompts* and little signs of encouragement to help the other person to continue talking. Nod your head in an affirmative way (without signifying your approval of what they are saying) and use facial expressions which reflect the nature of the other person's remarks.

An open and receptive *body posture* helps the other person to talk freely and feel less defensive. Face the other person in a natural way and don't put up barriers by folding your arms or crossing your legs. Lean forward slightly in an alert posture to show your interest in what they are saying.

Encourage the other person to open up further and speak more fluently by using *verbal prompts*, such as 'yes', 'go on' and 'tell me some more'. Use a well-modulated voice with a consistent tone and pattern which is reassuring and comforting. Repeat a key word in a sentence if you think it will help to stimulate further remarks.

Be aware that the *setting* in which your listening takes place is vital. Ensure an atmosphere of privacy and eliminate distractions such as phone calls or other people walking into the room. Tell those who need to know that you must not be disturbed and make it clear to the other person that you have done that. Make sure that there are no desks or other barriers between you and always sit at the same level as the other person.

Learn to overcome the *barriers* to good listening. Don't let yourself be irritated by any words or expressions which the other person uses. Do not switch off, even though you think the other person is talking balderdash. If they say something which is contrary to your beliefs, swallow hard, control your facial expression and continue to encourage them with your body language.

Whilst this may seem like a lengthy recital of some difficult problems, they're not as bad as they seem! Since, however, good listening is such a crucial element in liberating leadership, it does pay to be aware of all the potential problems, so that you can overcome them.

✓ **Listening checklist**

- Make sure that you use active listening
- Practise concentrating on what the other person is saying
- Follow the other person's train of thought
- Tune in to the other person's emotions and feelings
- Remember to say as little as possible yourself and to let the other person do the talking
- Summarise regularly!
- Ask questions from time to time to clarify the information you are getting
- Develop the skills to enable you to give non-verbal encouragement and prompts
- Be aware of the importance of body posture and always use an open and receptive posture
- Use verbal prompts according to the circumstances
- Be aware of the importance of the setting and arrange matters so that everything possible is done to help the conversation
- Remember that there are numerous pitfalls and barriers to good listening which can be encountered

---

Innovation tips for liberating leaders

You, as a successful liberating leader, will need innovative skills, not only to be energetically creative and capable of generating stimulating initiatives but also so that you can encourage your staff to develop and deploy their own innovative skills.

Encourage initiative and innovation through examples. If people have been used to a regime where initiative has been frowned upon, they may 'need permission' to begin thinking for themselves. Some good examples of successful initiatives will help to prompt them.

As a liberating climate takes hold, people often become readier to talk and make suggestions. In conversation one day, a packing-line operator said to the Production Director: 'It'd be a lot better if we stacked these tubes the other way round, you know.' The Director replied: 'Seems a good idea – why don't you do it?' At which the operator seemed a little nonplussed and asked: 'Are we allowed to do that?' This example illustrates that a liberating climate cannot be created overnight – it takes time to mature and you have to work at it continuously. People need encouragement to speak, to share their thoughts and to come forward with ideas.

You must emphasise that innovations need not be major ones. Small improvements – modifications in the way goods are handled, a different procedure – all are helpful and all show people that they can join in and contribute.

Make sure that you publicise and celebrate the initiatives that people come up with, and encourage others by using examples. Once the ball starts rolling, you'll find that a lot more thought is given to new ideas. You may find that your informal plugging of initiative and innovation is sufficient and that you get the ideas flowing. Even if you only elicit a few, the fact that people can contribute adds to the feeling that the organisational environment has become a healthy, energetic and creative one.

Be aware of all the negative emotions about the use of initiative. In some organisations there is a natural tendency to view any new idea, especially one that comes from 'below', with suspicion. You need to be aware of this and to urge that ideas of all kinds are welcome.

Don't make it difficult for people to contribute. Ensure that people can get their ideas straight to a decision-making point in the organisation – they should not have to go through several other layers first, with the consequent dangers of delay and frustration.

Don't ask other sections, departments or individuals to challenge or criticise a new idea. If you share someone's idea around, it should be in a positive spirit, not a negative one. Ask others to build on the idea, develop it, come up with variants, or polish it until it can be put into practice.

If managers treat problems as signs of failure, people will soon start to cover up when equipment or procedures are not working properly.

If you encourage the sharing of information, however, and treat mistakes as opportunities, the green shoots of initiative will appear.

Be open about any possible changes in structures or methods which might be under discussion.

Liberating leadership is incompatible with any attempt to alter a departmental routine in a secretive way or to spring changes on people unexpectedly. If you are secretive with them, they'll be secretive with you and all initiatives will be stillborn.

In an organisation with a liberating leadership and a well-established liberating climate, such negative attitudes will not exist and initiative will be encouraged and rewarded.

As a leader, however, it is up to you to reflect, through your own actions and example, the great importance which you and your organisation attach to initiative and innovation.

✓ Innovation checklist

- Encourage innovation in every way you can
- Pass on examples of good ideas which have been adopted, and tell people where the ideas came from
- Remember that you'll have to work at encouraging initiative and that it may be some time before everyone is comfortable with the concept
- Go for the small improvements and initiatives and give them plenty of praise
- Once it starts, keep the ball rolling!
- Challenge people to make improvements if they can
- Use targets if you think it's appropriate
- Celebrate initiatives, improvements and innovations whenever you can
- Always make it clear that you're open to new ideas
- Never be too busy to talk about new ideas, whether they ultimately prove to be practicable or not
- If you commit yourself to a new idea, stay committed
- Always be positive
- Never say: 'That won't work!'

L = LIBERATES

LIBERATING LEADER BEHAVIOURS

Does not blame people for mistakes

Encourages the people closest to the job to take their own

decisions

Listens to their staff

Encourages full and open communication

Operates systems based on trust, rather than suspicion

Encourages staff to develop new ideas

LIBERATING LEADER ATTRIBUTES

A belief that everyone can contribute

A belief that individuals can grow and develop

A belief that people respond to encouragement

A belief that people should be trusted

A liking for people

Openness and frankness

Fairness

LIBERATING LEADER SKILLS AND COMPETENCIES

Coaching skills

Providing encouragement to others

Creating a 'blame-free' environment

LISTENING SKILLS

THE PROMOTION OF INNOVATION

CHAPTER 4

E means 'encourages and supports'

The second letter of our slogan LEADER is 'E' for ENCOURAGES AND SUPPORTS. Thus the second characteristic of the liberating leader is that he or she *encourages and supports* others.

In order to encourage someone, managers, leaders or manager-leaders need to build up that person's self-esteem, assisting them to develop their own self-confidence. Successes should be praised and mistakes treated constructively. Other staff should not be ridiculed or humiliated when mistakes are under discussion.

Liberating leaders need to demonstrate that they have faith in other people by not interfering unnecessarily, by persuading them to take their own decisions and by giving them increasingly challenging tasks. The ideas and suggestions of others should always be treated seriously.

Liberating leaders must be available to support people by listening to their concerns and problems and by providing direction and guidance. They should keep their eyes open for signs of unhealthy stress and act to minimise it.

The profile of 'encourages and supports'

If YOU are going to become a liberating leader, then you need to make sure that you can ENCOURAGE AND SUPPORT. This means, as the LEADER Profile indicates:

- accepting responsibility for the actions of your staff
- giving praise where it is due
- recognising, and acting to minimise, other people's stress
- supporting your staff when they need support
- regularly meeting with individuals to clarify direction
- making people feel important and showing that you have faith in them.

You need to look at each of these in more detail, but remember that they are not necessarily separate and distinct aspects of behaviour. Rather, they represent a 'portfolio' of behaviours which you will need to use.

Accepting responsibility for the actions of your staff

Some managers and leaders do not believe that they should accept any responsibility for the actions of their staff; they expect job-holders to follow instructions, to perform tasks correctly and to act properly at all times. Liberating leadership, on the other hand, establishes a climate of collaboration within the organisation. You need to assist this process by ensuring that responsibility and accountability are shared and spread within your own sphere of influence. As responsibilities are devolved, both individuals and teams will assume greater ownership of their actions.

At the same time, however, leadership involves taking responsibility for others. The truly liberated organisation will develop a comprehensive network of interconnecting responsibilities. You have to be able to accept full responsibility for the actions of your own staff.

Giving praise where it is due

Leaders and managers often find it difficult to give praise. Although you will be keen to give praise where it is due, it may still present some difficulties. It is one of those managerial activities which seems simpler at first sight than it later actually proves to be.

The key phrase is 'where it is due'. A leader who praises simple activities too fulsomely, or who fails to distinguish between different tasks and praises everything in an indiscriminate manner, will soon lose credibility.

**'I've got all the managers saying "please" and "thank
you" now – it helps a lot more than you might think.'**

Production Manager

You should learn to give praise in a straightforward way, so that the
recipient recognises that praise is being given and that encouragement
and support is being provided. In time, both parties understand the
strength of the praise being proffered, so that it acquires real value as a
mark of the leader's support.

Recognising, and acting to minimise, other people's stress
Leaders from the older managerial traditions may not recognise stress,
or its effects, let alone consider how to minimise it. For a leader with
this simplistic approach, poor performance means only that the
individual concerned has failed to achieve the standards required and
must improve. The causes of such a deterioration are not on the agenda
for the 'unliberating' manager.

**'Giving people some of my responsibility doesn't mean
giving them some of my stress!'**

Managing Director

You, on the other hand, will acknowledge that stress is a genuine factor
in the work environment and that it must be taken seriously as a
potential inhibitor of performance. You will recognise the forms in
which it occurs and its symptoms, and try to ensure that your staff are
not subjected to the kinds of stress that can reduce performance to the
detriment of the organisation.

Supporting your staff when they need support
Some of the more traditional managers and leaders maintain an 'arm's
length' relationship with their staff, thereby steering clear of any
problems that individuals might encounter. They consider that staff are
simply there to do a job and they expect them to do it – literally with
no questions asked.

You, however, as a liberating leader practising E FOR ENCOURAGES AND SUPPORTS, will recognise that there are circumstances where individuals encounter problems which affect their performance, whether work-related or personal. You must be a natural supporter of your staff, aware that words of help and support can bridge the gap for an individual until they are able to overcome their problems.

> **'It helps to demonstrate your support with something tangible. If you can provide them with some new gear or a bit of equipment, that's a lot better than just standing there saying "I'm right behind you!"'**
>
> *Maintenance Manager*

Regularly meeting with individuals to clarify direction

You will be aware that many managers and leaders do not feel the need to clarify matters with staff: their managerial methods often involve telling the troops what to do and making sure that they get on with it.

You, however, will take a contrary view – a liberating leadership view. The performance of any individual will be enhanced if there is mutual agreement and understanding between manager and team member about what is being done, how it is being done and the direction in which the team, section or department is heading.

Making people feel important and showing that you have faith in them

Whilst some leaders may be reluctant to accept that people need to feel important, you, as a liberating leader, will make people feel important in a variety of thoughtful ways. In addition, you will indicate, whenever you can, that you have faith in each individual and are confident that he or she can deliver good performances.

Recognising that many people tend to fulfil the expectations that others have of them, if you can make it clear to individuals that you expect a high level of performance from them, they will respond. By offering them suitable encouragement and support, you will build up their self-esteem and help them to perform better.

There will be many opportunities to build the self-esteem of others by using a simple and straightforward approach. Greet people warmly, use their correct names and show a genuine interest in them. Indicate respect by not invading their personal space, keeping a comfortable level of eye contact and adopting a relaxed stance. Show genuine pleasure (and not surprise!) when another person demonstrates superior skill or knowledge. Hold lively meetings which enable everyone to contribute. Don't use jargon or long words which might confuse people or put them down. Get actively involved at shopfloor level. Initiate and join regular celebrations of achievements. Smile!

Your attributes, skills and competencies

The six behaviours which characterise E FOR ENCOURAGES AND SUPPORTS are underpinned by particular attributes, skills or competencies which you, as a liberating leader, will need to use. We end this chapter by examining two of these, which you may need to extend or develop: **communication skills** and **recognising and dealing with stress in others**.

Communication: tips for liberating leaders

Good liberating leaders have to be good communicators. To be effective in a modern, open environment, you must have the full range of communication skills. Managerial communication penetrates every aspect of corporate life and should be mastered by anyone who aspires to effective leadership. It involves the spoken and the written word; the simple and the complex; the set-piece speech to an attentive, assembled audience and the brief word exchanged in a corridor; the formal and the informal; the direct and the indirect; the recorded and the unrecorded.

You will need to be skilled in having face-to-face communication with

- **individuals**, either in their own workspace, where they are relaxed and comfortable, or in other environments, where they may be less relaxed and sometimes actually uncomfortable
- **small groups**, either gathered informally or perhaps convened for an official team-briefing session

- **large groups**, perhaps with people drawn from right across the organisation, presenting an audience of considerable diversity
- **selected gatherings of individuals**, with whom you can talk and who can then pass on the information to the various sections they represent.

You also need to be skilled in the use of all kinds of written communication. Now some people are naturally good at face-to-face communication, but have less facility with the written word. For other people the reverse may be true. It is human nature to prefer the methods with which you are most comfortable, but for effective liberating leadership you must master all forms of communication.

When you deliver information on a face-to-face basis, you convey far more to people than if you were merely to write up your script for 'publication'. When people can see and hear you, they are evaluating your performance on a continuous basis: your credibility, and therefore the 'value' of the information you are imparting, is at stake.

For that reason, informal face-to-face communication has a risk attached to it. You might fail. You might be 'shown up'. Your script, whilst precise and pertinent as words, could be undermined by the way you present it to your audience. That is why some managers, recognising the risk of failure, fall back on the safer option of the written word. The written word, they say to themselves, is safe and cannot be misunderstood.

Liberating leaders, on the other hand, realise that if they can get it right, they will get much more information across and achieve their message. Whilst the written word may be safer, the opportunities for successful communication and for making the right impact are so much greater with personal contact.

Since liberating leadership must be positive leadership, the choice is clear: use face-to-face communication and make sure you become good at it. If you learn how to do it and practise it regularly, you'll eliminate the risk, improve your standing and ensure that your message gets across to all.

Communication is not just about getting *your* message over – that's only half of it! You can only create a truly liberating environment if you both give and receive information with equal freedom and understanding. Throughout your organisation there should be many open channels of two-way communication, through which information flows freely. The rigidities of the old hierarchical systems often prevented proper communication taking place and could deny information to the very people who actually needed it. Liberating an organisation means setting it free and thereby releasing all the necessary information.

For the liberating leader who is seeking excellence in communications, two particular attributes must be developed: the ability to walk the job effectively and to understand and use a variety of questioning techniques.

Walking the job

It is essential for anyone who has a managerial or a leadership role to be visible in that role. If the leader is seen around the organisation every day and demonstrates that he or she is in active touch with what is going on, credibility and respect benefit enormously. A remote leader cannot be a good leader.

When you walk the job it must not represent some temporary escape from your in-tray, or some ritual set-piece you have taught yourself to perform. It must be an integral part of your managerial leadership and you must do it purposefully: to learn, to inform, to stimulate, to inspire and to celebrate.

As with other techniques, you'll have to practise 'managing by wandering around' to get the best out of it. Go at different times, visit sections in different sequences, move rapidly, move slowly. Chat to people. Find out about them as individuals. Be relaxed. Smile. Laugh. Encourage people. Congratulate people. Sympathise with people. Go with the flow.

As you practise all this, however, you will be acquiring information – about individuals, about problems, about success, about failure, about an everyday story of organisational folk. You will have your finger on the pulse and you'll be listening to the heartbeat of your organisation. And people in turn will, of course, be learning more about you.

You will find that much of the information you glean does not have to be used there and then. Indeed, you may think that some of it does not have a use at all, but store it up, because one day it might. You'll be able to pull out a little plum of information which will help to encourage someone, assist with teambuilding, point up a valuable message or contribute to an improved performance.

Questioning – the vital skill

If you're involved in a difficult discussion session and you don't get the right answers, it can be argued with some justification that you have not asked the right questions! A good communicator will use a flexible range of different types of questions. In most of the situations which you face, you will have to discover facts and establish feelings by using a combination of the following sorts of question:

Open questions

Open questions enable you to gain more information. Typically, they begin with one of the six words immortalised by Rudyard Kipling in his poem *The Serving-men*:

> I keep six honest serving-men
> (They taught me all I knew);
> Their names are *What* and *Why* and *When*
> And *How* and *Where* and *Who*.[1]

In addition to these famous six, you can also use as an opening: 'Tell me about ...' Use these open questions to get the other person to talk about ideas and feelings as well as about facts.

Closed questions

Closed questions invite a simple answer of finality, such as 'yes' or 'no'. They often start with words like 'Can you ...?' or 'Will you ...?' or 'Is it ...?' or 'Do you ...?' Do not be misled, perhaps by something you may have read or been told, into believing that open questions are *good* and closed questions are *bad*. Closed questions may be used quite correctly and effectively for certain purposes. It is a matter of fitting the type of question to the circumstances.

Closed questions may be useful if you are summarising and want

[1] *Author's italics*

someone to agree or disagree with your summary. They can also be used to return to the subject in hand if the conversation has wandered, and they prove useful when checking if you have understood correctly. Above all, they are essential when you need to establish or confirm facts.

Specific questions

Specific questions incorporate pointers that enable you to home in on particular information in a sharper way. Thus, instead of 'When did you first notice this?', you can ask: 'On what date did you first notice this?'

Specific questions are needed when you have to find out the exact facts of a situation or when you want to steer a rambling conversation towards useful intelligence.

Reflective questions

Reflective questions are used for rephrasing what has been said and returning it as a question. An example would be: 'You're saying that you feel this decision was incorrect?' It reflects, as accurately as possible, what the other person has said. You do not need to endorse it, just represent it. Used appropriately, it encourages the other person to expand on the subject and to give you more information.

In an important modification of this, you can use a reflective technique which provides the other person with a return statement rather than a question. In our example, the words would be the same, but the rising inflection in the voice which indicates a question would be absent. This allows you to concentrate fully on the other person's meaning without seeming to cross-question them.

You should indicate your interest in what the other person is saying (particularly if it is of a personal or sensitive nature) without showing any bias or revealing your own views. Your remarks should be prefaced initially by phrases such as 'you feel', 'you think', or 'it seems to you that', but as the conversation develops these can be dropped.

You will find that these reflecting techniques are a very useful way of checking up on what someone means if you are unsure. It helps you to establish rapport, because it does not cut across the other person's thought processes, whilst at the same time indicating your understanding of what they are saying.

Communication checklist

- Make sure you're effective at the full range of communicating skills
- Whenever you can, communicate face to face with people
- Be aware of the communication methods you prefer, then work hard to brush up on the other methods
- Remember that communication is a two-way process: make sure you're always receiving as well as transmitting
- Encourage everyone to communicate effectively
- Use walking the job as one of your communication techniques
- Work hard to become skilled in the use of questioning techniques
- Use open questions whenever you can and whenever they're appropriate
- Remember that closed questions are not banned: they can be essential in some circumstances
- Use specific questions judiciously as you need to
- Remember that reflective questions can help you when you need to clarify certain facts or remain neutral

Stress reduction: tips for liberating leaders

Recognising stress

Stress can be an important ingredient in any organisational mix. As a liberating leader, you will need to be able to manage stress, which will mean heightening your awareness of what stress is and how it can be recognised. Three forms of stress have been identified as a result of detailed observations of behaviour:

UNDERSTRESS HEALTHY STRESS OVERSTRESS

The traditional stress curve, shown in Figure 5, illustrates understress, healthy stress and overstress and their relationship with performance. Because each person is an individual, their own curve will have its own specific outline, but the general form and shape of the curve is common to all of us and enables a number of general conclusions to be drawn.

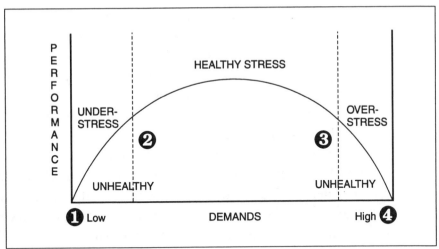

Fig. 5. The stress curve

If we feel too little stress, our effectiveness at that time will reflect our under-stimulation and be reduced. We are all aware of those moments when we are bored or lethargic, have no enthusiasm for the day or the job and feel unmotivated or frustrated. Perhaps we do not have enough demands, or the work is too easy. The expressions, commonly heard, that 'I work better under pressure' or 'I give my best work when the heat's on' encapsulate this *understress*. In such circumstances we sometimes generate greater pressure for ourselves by leaving a tight deadline for a project and then having to pull out all the stops to complete it – giving an enhanced performance in the process.

As our stress increases, our energy generally rises and our performance grows until we reach our optimum stimulation. In this part of the curve, we are performing at our absolute peak. We feel stimulated, excited and challenged by the opportunities presented by a demand, in control and with the right amount of variety and change for us. This is when we deliver our best work. We are in *healthy stress* and feel at our most satisfied.

If this goes on for too long, however, we become overstretched and overstimulated, and our performance can diminish. We begin to feel that the demands are too great, that we cannot fulfil our commitments – and our feeling becomes reality as we experience *overstress*. We may begin to behave in ways that sabotage our performance. Perhaps we

procrastinate, pick arguments, work exceptionally long hours, delegate
ineffectively, have difficulties in sleeping, or sleep too much and fail
to view things with our normal clarity.

What are the actual warning signs which help us to identify where
a given person may stand on this stress curve? How do we know, as
we observe a colleague, whether they are experiencing understress,
healthy stress or overstress?

The three lists which follow indicate the tell-tale behavioural signs
which characterise the three kinds of stress. You will see that the lists
are extensive, but of course a given individual may only exhibit a few
characteristics. They will not follow a set pattern, but they can be very
useful indicators. What you must watch out for is *change*, because any
alteration in a person's customary behaviour should alert you to a
potential problem.

Signs of UNDERSTRESS

- low self-esteem
- tiredness
- irritability
- critical attitude
- unreliability
- disgruntled manner
- lack of decision-making
- makes simple errors
- irregular attendance
- little interest in work
- confused thinking
- lower energy
- slowness
- lack of enthusiasm
- takes excess of stimulants

Signs of HEALTHY STRESS

- good concentration
- sense of humour
- cooperative
- enhanced achievements
- high standards
- strong interest in job
- effective problem-solving
- good long-term planning
- deadlines met
- high motivation
- clear thinking
- positive comments
- confident decision-making
- constructive criticism given and received
- good timekeeping
- good attendance record
- concern and care for others
- harmonious relationships

You should make yourself familiar with the content of these lists (Signs of Overstress list is overleaf) and keep close observation on people, so that if you detect any symptoms of understress or overstress, you can take appropriate action. Whilst there are similarities between the understress and the overstress symptoms, your investigation will soon reveal which cause is involved. You will find that an individual's capacity to cope with stress at work varies according to the state of their private life, their confidence that they have the support of the organisation and their control over their surroundings.

Signs of OVERSTRESS

- lack of concentration
- taking work home
- memory losses
- disgruntled
- poor decision-making
- uncooperative relationships
- worry, anxiety or fear
- poor work quality
- depression
- emotional outbursts
- inconsistency
- not meeting targets or deadlines
- irregular attendance and timekeeping
- unpredictability
- low self-esteem
- tiredness
- ineffective problem-solving
- over self-critical
- extreme mood swings
- customer complaints
- accidents
- poor long-term planning
- eating difficulties
- lost orders
- sleep problems
- no sense of humour
- low interest in work

✔ **Stress reduction checklist**

- Make yourself familiar with the shape of the stress curve
- Become thoroughly conversant with the different features of understress, healthy stress and overstress
- Familiarise yourself with the signs and pointers which can indicate that a person is experiencing understress, healthy stress or overstress
- If and when action is needed, find ways to adjust the stress being experienced by the person under review

E = ENCOURAGES AND SUPPORTS

LIBERATING LEADER BEHAVIOURS

Accepts responsibility for the actions of their staff

Gives praise where it is due

Recognises, and acts to minimise, other people's stress

Supports staff when they need support

Regularly meets with individuals to clarify direction

Makes people feel important and shows that they have faith in them

LIBERATING LEADER ATTRIBUTES

A belief that people need support and help

A belief that individuals must be shown that they are valued

A belief that everyone can have good ideas

Accepts responsibility

A natural readiness to praise others

A sympathetic approach

LIBERATING LEADER SKILLS AND COMPETENCIES

One-to-one skills

Able to create a purposeful environment

COMMUNICATION SKILLS

ABLE TO RECOGNISE AND DEAL WITH STRESS

CHAPTER 5

A means 'achieves purpose'

The third letter of our slogan LEADER is 'A' for ACHIEVES PURPOSE. Thus, the third characteristic of the liberating leader is that he or she *achieves the purpose of* the particular team, group, section, department, company or organisation.

In any competitive marketplace, a manager or leader who cannot achieve effective and consistent results will risk not only their own continuity of employment but also the security of those they have to lead. Inevitably, this can mean that there are occasions when the liberating leader has to take difficult and unpopular decisions in order to reach agreed objectives and targets.

Liberating leaders should ask for the views of the people they lead before taking a decision which affects them. Such consultation gives rise to a better quality of decision and produces one which the others are more likely to be able to support.

It is essential that the liberating leader, together with the people they lead, are totally clear about their purpose. This purpose is, after all, one of the factors that gives the team its strength and unity. A vision of what the team is aiming for will paint a picture of the future which can inspire and unite people.

Such a vision cannot be the leader's alone: it must be a shared vision. Each team, section or department should be clear about their vision.

Liberating leaders must live the vision and use every opportunity to remind people, face to face, of its importance.

The profile of 'achieves purpose'

If YOU are going to become a liberating leader, then you need to make sure that you can ACHIEVE PURPOSE. This means, as the LEADER Profile indicates:

- achieving results
- agreeing demanding targets with individuals or teams
- consulting those affected before making decisions
- being willing to take unpopular decisions in order to move forward
- seeking out future challenges and opportunities
- regularly communicating an inspirational view of the future
- constantly seeking to improve the way things are done

You need to look at each of these seven behaviours in more detail, remembering that together they form the 'portfolio' of behaviours which you, as a liberating leader, can use to help you and your team achieve your purpose.

You should be aware, however, that there is a greater degree of potential conflict associated with this segment of the slogan. The main thrust of the leadership activities and actions listed here is to 'get things done'. The liberating leader, just like a non-liberating leader, has to keep things moving forward.

Clearly, the desire to drive for results could come into conflict with the need to nurture and sustain a liberating atmosphere. You may have to take difficult decisions when consultation does not produce consensus. In a major crisis, you will have to make rapid decisions: the urgency of the situation might not allow all the liberating refinements.

In promoting liberating leadership, however, consultation remains vital. A liberating climate is a positive factor, not a negative one, even when difficult decisions loom. For it is only by utilising that liberating climate, carefully created and fostered by a responsible and caring leader, that those really tough decisions can be made and implemented effectively.

Even in a carefully nurtured climate of liberation, you may have to make unpopular decisions. If there has been consultation, explanation, discussion and communication, however, these decisions should be more readily accepted by those who are affected. Such a decision may remain unpopular, but it will be accepted. By contrast, a leader in an 'unliberated' organisation could find that an unpopular decision is never accepted and becomes a festering sore which interferes with the achievement of purpose.

So this group of behaviours, whilst carrying certain tensions, can remain compatible. You, as a leader who intends to learn and practise liberating leadership, will find these activities a valuable and necessary part of your liberating toolbox.

Achieving results

There is no doubt that 'achieving results' is the *raison d'être* of the manager and the leader. The public perception of the leader is of a go-getter – someone who has drive, someone who makes things happen, someone who ensures that there is a forward momentum in the organisation. In that traditional picture, it is the leader who gets the results. For the liberating leader, however, it is different. You are responsible for making things happen, but you have to do that by liberating others. You can achieve your results and contribute to the results of your section, team or department, but the whole point of a liberating approach is that everyone becomes liberated to achieve results.

There are many examples in sport where the team captain is not the team's most skilful or effective individual player. His or her leadership, however, brings the best out of the other players: he or she *liberates* the skills and effectiveness of the others in the team. So it can be with you and your organisational team.

'Now that everybody is singing from the same hymn-sheet, we feel we can achieve anything and everything.'

Training and Development Manager

You, as a liberating leader practising A FOR ACHIEVES PURPOSE, will recognise that a hard-edged reality and a need for difficult choices must permeate your role. The difference between you and those who practise more traditional styles will lie in the way that you tackle that reality and make those choices. You will use your liberating and democratic style to achieve exactly the same ends – and because you can harness the collaborative power of all, you will achieve more meaningful and sustainable results.

Agreeing demanding targets with individuals or teams
You will recognise that, under a liberating leadership approach, the only certain method for establishing effective targets must involve people proposing their own goals and signalling their commitment. You will use the techniques of liberating leadership to ensure that consultations and discussions lead to agreement about demanding but attainable targets. The spirit of collaboration and harmony which is engendered by a liberating atmosphere will increase the effectiveness of the targets and the probability of success.

Consulting those affected before making decisions
Managers and leaders with a less liberating style tend not to consult others, unless, perhaps, they are forced to do so by legislation. They make decisions and stick to them. Other people have no influence over the decisions made, nor any say about their impact.

Under that kind of regime, decisions are simply 'handed down'. Orders are given and the revised situation takes immediate effect: there is no question of contesting a decision which has already been taken. Those who serve under such leadership experience its remoteness: a deliberate distancing and an avoidance of contact with those who are left to implement the decisions.

'They seem to have realised that I know a bit about the job – I've only been doing it for twenty years!'

Process Technician

You, however, will recognise that the people who are affected by decisions need to be consulted. You will understand that if a decision, or proposed decision, is going to have a direct impact upon the way an individual or a group work, that individual or group must be consulted fully and comprehensively. A climate of liberating leadership ensures that each issue is considered and discussed close to the point in the organisation where it has most impact.

You will also know that there are instances where a decision has an indirect effect upon an individual or group. It may not specifically change the way they work, but it will have some impact upon the organisation and they will have to take account of that. Such people must also be consulted appropriately, even though the process may not need to be as comprehensive as in the other case.

You need to manage the consultation process properly. There should be no sense of 'going through the motions'. At the end of the process, the proposed decision may still go ahead unmodified, or it may be amended or dropped. Whatever the outcome, both you as a liberating leader and the others should feel that the process has been fair and that the effects will strengthen the organisation.

Being willing to take unpopular decisions in order to move forward
You must be willing to take unpopular decisions in order to move forward. You will recognise, however, that with a proper process of consultation and a true climate of liberating leadership, there is a good chance that the decisions will be less unpopular than they might otherwise have been, and that, over time, their unpopularity will diminish.

> **'This company used to be far too slow to react to our customers. Now everybody accepts that we've got to move fast to stay in business.'**
>
> *Sales Manager*

Seeking out future challenges and opportunities
Those managers and leaders who work in a rigid style usually ensure the perpetuation of the *status quo*. The organisation continues to

function, but it has an inherent inflexibility which makes it shy away from challenges and miss opportunities.

> **'We're always ready to do things a bit differently if it helps to satisfy the customer.'**
>
> *Production Director*

You, on the other hand, are a liberating leader. The flexible, democratic and consultative climate in which you operate does not shirk challenges and welcomes opportunities. Once again, a liberating atmosphere makes the achievement of purpose more likely. Through teamwork, through your involvement with people as individuals, through discussion and debate, you will encourage everyone to identify the challenges that lie ahead and devise ways of tackling them.

You should help people to see that their organisation can never stand still and that challenges and opportunities are two sides of the same coin. If you face continued challenges, you may begin to feel that change is being forced upon you and that you are reacting to events rather than controlling them. If this is the case, you must encourage everyone to think proactively and to seek opportunities for positive action.

Opportunities for change should be welcomed. A liberating atmosphere helps everyone to recognise opportunities as positive signs that the team can control events rather than be pushed around by them. You should use all your skills to encourage your people to use their initiative and *create* opportunities, rather than waiting for them to occur. Remember to 'accentuate the positive' at all times.

Regularly communicating an inspirational view of the future
Leaders who use a more traditional style do not always put over a clear view of how they see the future. They may well have such a view, but they don't communicate it to other people in an effective way.

You will consider that the communication of a vision of the future is essential to the achievement of purpose. A liberating climate will draw people together and provide a much greater sense of common purpose for everyone in the organisation. That purpose will be strengthened further if everyone has a shared sense of the aims and objectives and can visualise what the future holds for them. You will endeavour to present your vision in an inspiring way and to communicate it in a variety of different forms at intervals, so that the message is continuously reinforced.

> **'When I first started talking about a vision, they thought I'd got religion. Now they all say it – the word's part of their vocabulary.'**
>
> *Managing Director*

Constantly seeking to improve the way things are done
You will seek continuous improvement through a process of consultation and collaboration. In addition, because you have created a liberating climate, you will find that continuous improvement will spring naturally from within the organisation, instead of having to be prised out of it.

Your attributes, skills and competencies

The seven behaviours which characterise A FOR ACHIEVES PURPOSE are underpinned by particular attributes, skills or competencies which you, as a liberating leader, will need to use.

Two of these, in particular, you may need to extend or develop: **target-setting skills** and the **skills of visioning**.

Target-setting: tips for liberating leaders

Targets are priorities or special tasks which need to be achieved. They relate specifically to an individual, to a section or workgroup, to a department or to a complete organisation. Targets are concerned with changes, with development and with the improvement of performance. Targets involve short-term alterations in performance, whereas standards are continuing yardsticks.

Targets must be established, but *you* will not establish those targets alone. Your first priority will be to consult with your staff. If an individual understands his or her job fully, then he or she will be able to propose suitable targets which you can endorse.

The setting of good, effective, challenging targets should always be the responsibility of well-informed and experienced people who know the complexities of the job – and who better than the job-holder?

Joint target-setting can help you to improve team performance, both in terms of quality and quantity. Individuals need targets which will provide them with an aim and a purpose. The target will usually be set at some suitable point between the current individual level of performance and the best. Common sense is the best guide, so no performance target should be set unrealistically far above that of the present level. Since targets can be set and reset, the best plan is to try to 'edge-up' performance by using a sequence of tougher targets over a period of time.

Targets can also be used to develop skills, knowledge and competence. Individuals or teams can agree targets which specify the skills to be learned or perfected, or the knowledge to be acquired, or the competence to be developed. In this case, the 'little and often' principle is again very helpful, allowing people to use targets to raise their skills gradually to the levels required.

One further objective of target-setting, and a most useful one, is to provide a challenge and offer a threshold for a sense of achievement. Teams and individuals can set *ad hoc* challenges for themselves as particular situations arise.

Such targets can be a powerful stimulant and energiser and they are particularly relevant in a liberating climate, because they spring spontaneously from within workgroups, rather than from an imposed edict.

The targets which you agree with them will help people to contribute more effectively to their organisation by clarifying questions such as:

- What should I be doing?
- Whom do I work with?
- What standard is expected of me?
- How am I doing?
- Where do I go from here and how do I get there?

In the more dynamic climate created by liberating leadership, joint team target-setting becomes a natural consequence of the democratic approach to work. You will find that it is a very useful contributor to the greater clarity of purpose and openness which liberalisation brings.

Organisational target-setting requires a systematic routine whereby the parties concerned (yourself, as the liberating leader, and an individual, or yourself and a team) regularly review performance and set targets for a forthcoming period. Set this up by agreement with everyone involved.

There are four prerequisites which need to be in place before your target-setting can take place with an individual or a team. These are:

● a sound organisational structure
● realistic lines of accountability
● a comprehensive statement of the relevant responsibilities
● agreed standards of performance.

You need to ensure that all four are established and agreed before moving on to the target-setting process.

Keep your targets simple and advise a job-holder or team not to have more than five or six specified targets. They will not be able to concentrate on or cope with more than that, and the likelihood of sustained success will thus be reduced.

Target-setting is about dialogue and mutual commitment rather than paperwork. It is important, however, to keep accurate and effective records about performance against targets. You may be worried that this could herald a return to the old command and control days, but it should not do so. A liberating climate is an open one; and open records are part of that pattern.

Target-setting checklist

- Be clear about the objectives of target-setting
- Use targets flexibly, for a number of different purposes
- Remember that using targets can help to underpin liberation by affording greater clarity of purpose and more openness
- Use a proper systematic routine for your target-setting
- Bring targets into play once you have the organisational structure, the agreed responsibilities, the clear accountabilities and the standards of performance properly in place
- Keep your targets simple
- Ensure that there are no ambiguities or inconsistencies
- Use a few clear and straightforward targets rather than a lot of complicated ones
- Keep open and effective records to monitor your targets
- Review the effectiveness of your target-setting process regularly

Visioning: tips for liberating leaders

Liberating leaders are effective leaders: effective leaders are successful. In order for you to be successful it is essential that you have a clear picture of the direction you are taking, why you are taking it and what things will be like along the road.

Leading, whether it be a team, section, department, company or multinational group, cannot be achieved without vision. Attempting to lead without it is like trying to drive down a six-lane motorway in a violent rainstorm when your windscreen wipers have failed.

Leaders who prove to be without vision can soon reduce their team or section to a group of aimless, uninspired and lethargic also-rans. Leaders who can't come up with the vision will never come up with the goods.

As a liberating leader, you must be clear about the requirements of your role as a leader, whether it be in relation to an organisation, a department or team. You need to develop and share a simple statement of the 'business' you are in, and why you are in it.

Whilst a simple statement is the aim, it can often prove complicated to produce one. Identifying the business can present more problems than you think. Many corporate statements of purpose have been unwieldy and cumbersome – making them difficult for people to identify with.

There are certain key questions that should be asked when formulating a statement of purpose, or a *mission statement* as it is often called:

- *Say to yourself*: what is our real business? (Sometimes, this can be a more difficult question to answer than it appears at first sight.)
- *Say to yourself*: who are our customers? Who are the people you really need to satisfy?
- *Say to yourself*: where are our customers? Are they internal customers, external customers, or both? Are they in the UK, or in the EU, or in both? Do they exist worldwide?
- *Say to yourself*: what is our value to our customers? Where does it lie? Does it lie in providing the cheapest? Or in providing the fastest? Or in providing the most reliable?

A study by Ashridge Management College of the mission statements of 200 UK organisations concluded that 'organisations with a sense of mission can capture the emotional support of their people'. So clarity of mission, encapsulated in a clear statement of that mission, is an essential element in any organisation which wants to practise liberating leadership.

The second key area for liberating leaders is to develop a vision of what can be achieved by the organisation, department, team or any other sub-unit. You need to create a mental picture of an improved operation, or a better business or a smarter way of working.

You must create and hold this vision and then share it with the organisation, making sure that your communication is for internal consumption only. Don't make the mistake of publicising your vision externally – it might be seen (unfairly, perhaps) as a public relations stunt.

Your vision should call for change or improvement of some kind: it would be rather feeble to have a vision of the *status quo*. Take care, however, that your picture of change or improvement is not represented (or misrepresented) as adverse comment upon your colleagues and the organisation as a whole. Your vision should look to the future, but it should also carry people forward into that future by making them feel that they are worthwhile.

As you begin to develop and refine your vision, you may find that it does not seem wholly credible to others in the light of prevailing circumstances or their current experiences. So be prepared to work away at it so that you can then share it with your colleagues and be confident that it is robust enough to meet any challenges they may want to make.

Visions should inspire people to want to improve or change the work or the way they do it. Your vision, properly communicated, should help to reinforce the commitment that a liberating climate initiates.

Remember that it is entirely natural for people to feel diffident, sceptical or short of confidence when they first hear about 'vision'. The concept is a strange one for them, so they will express their doubts, but you should meet these by listening carefully, by explaining and clarifying and then by challenging them where necessary.

Change, development and improvement within organisations is not a consequence of revised systems and procedures: it occurs because people actually want to contribute to the success or improvement of their part of the organisation. This 'will' does not just happen, but it can be born out of a shared picture of something better, more exciting, more interesting or more rewarding.

When you prepare your statement of purpose and vision, make sure that it is:

- inspiring
- empowering
- clear and challenging
- driving towards excellence
- compatible with your market
- likely to stand the test of time
- a beacon to guide people
- a preparation for the future, but a link with the past.

Your statement will wither and die if it is treated as merely a paper exercise. It is essential for you to 'walk your talk', by getting out there with people, reminding them of the vision and continuing to paint the 'big picture'. You don't need large-scale, slick presentations. But you do need to be in all the various workspaces, using one or two key phrases to constantly reinforce your message.

Remember that visions are not just about 'whole organisations'. They are even more relevant to sections, groups, teams and departments. It is important that these sub-areas support the vision and direction of the organisation: indeed, groups and teams can often help the top leadership to articulate their vision.

Visions need to be *inspirational*. Visions should be *motivational*. Visions ought to be *achievable*. Visions have to be *believable*.

Visions need to be dissected and repackaged so that they can be turned into tangible objectives which people feel they can tackle. Objectives have to be *specific*. Objectives need to be easily *understood*. Objectives should be widely *communicated*. Objectives must be *challenging*. Objectives ought to be *attainable*. Objectives will be *measurable*.

✔ Visioning checklist

- Always be certain about the direction you are taking
- Be clear about your own role as a leader
- Develop and share a mission statement about the business you are in
- Keep your mission statement simple!
- Think very carefully and clearly about your real business
- Think about your customers: who they are, where they are and what they value from you
- Develop a vision of what can be achieved by your organisation
- Be prepared to work on your vision to get it right
- Share your vision with the organisation
- Make your statement of vision positive and telling
- Share and reinforce your vision as you walk around the organisation, talking with your colleagues

A = ACHIEVES PURPOSE

LIBERATING LEADER BEHAVIOURS

Achieves results

Agrees demanding targets with individuals or teams

Consults those affected before making decisions

Is willing to take unpopular decisions in order to move forward

Seeks out future challenges/opportunities

Regularly communicates an inspirational view of the future

Constantly seeks to improve the way things are done

LIBERATING LEADER ATTRIBUTES

A belief that people must be consulted

A belief that challenges are there to be met

A belief that targets can help to produce results

Having vision and a clear view of the future

A clear and firm decision-maker

Results-oriented

LIBERATING LEADER SKILLS AND COMPETENCIES

Consultation skills

Effective decision-making

Able to foster continuous improvement

TARGET-SETTING SKILLS

COMMUNICATING A VISION OF THE FUTURE

CHAPTER 6

D means 'develops people and teams'

The fourth letter of our slogan LEADER is 'D' for DEVELOPS PEOPLE AND TEAMS. Thus the fourth skill area of the liberating leader is that he or she plays an essential role in *the development of individuals and teams*.

An organisation cannot grow if the people working for it do not. Liberating leaders invest time and effort in helping staff to develop themselves. They promote cross-training between team members and seek to set up effective coaching opportunities. They see it as part of their work to guide and coach their team and to act as a mentor to the individuals within it. Liberating leaders should be able to develop effective teams. Teamwork is a key to unlocking the talents and energy of the people in the organisation. Liberating leaders value and encourage diversity in order to provide the team with a strength and wholeness that would not otherwise exist.

The profile of 'develops people and teams'

If YOU are going to become a liberating leader, then you must be able to DEVELOP PEOPLE AND TEAMS. As the LEADER Profile indicates, this means:

● encouraging other people to learn
● encouraging people to work together as a team

- regularly meeting with the team, as a whole, to review progress
- taking time to develop and guide your staff
- dealing effectively with breaches in standards of behaviour
- treating other people's mistakes as learning opportunities.

Encouraging other people to learn

It is all too easy for some managers and leaders to give inadequate encouragement to others to learn. Their attitude is: they have their jobs, they should know how to perform them and they should keep on doing just that. Further learning may perhaps be considered either unnecessary or a cause of disruption.

You, however, will know that encouraging people to learn will lead to a higher standard of skill and expertise within the organisation that will generally be beneficial. Learning equips people with additional skills, but it also improves their confidence and makes them more self-reliant. A learning climate is a natural partner to a liberating climate.

> **'Training provides people with the ability to carry out particular procedures, but development gives them an understanding of the business and helps them to make effective decisions on their own.'**
>
> *Managing Director*

You will also recognise that when people are encouraged to learn more they do actually learn more. They then tend to perform better within their existing roles, enhancing the general level of performance and efficiency within the organisation. And, when encouraged to learn in one particular area, they frequently respond not just in that area, but in several others.

Encouraging people to work together as a team

As a liberating leader you will do all you can to encourage people to work together as a team. There is overwhelming evidence that well-motivated teams of people perform more effectively than do the sum of their individual parts.

Your encouragement of people to work together as a team should apply whatever the particular circumstances of your organisation. You may have a well-designed structure in which interlocking teams operate throughout the organisation; or you may have a few teams established in selected areas; alternatively, you may lack any tradition of formal teamworking altogether.

> **'Empowerment and teamworking are two sides of the same coin.'**
>
> *Personnel Manager*

If you have a situation where specific, designated teams are in operation, your encouragement should be directed towards keeping them on the right path and improving their working effectiveness further. If you have only a few teams in existence, you should encourage the formation of more.

Regularly meeting with the team, as a whole, to review progress
You will meet regularly with your whole team and use discussion as a practical instrument to assist development, improvement and progress. These meetings will form a natural and continuing process of furthering your mutual work activities. They will not be postponed, cancelled, shortened or interfered with, so that team members come to see them as a vital cog in the machinery of continuous improvement. Such progress reviews are yet another facet of a liberating climate that is beneficial to every part of the organisation.

Make a point, from time to time, of not taking the lead in your team meetings. If you encourage different members of the team to run the meetings on different occasions, you will find that this represents an excellent developmental technique for the individuals concerned and for the team as a whole.

> **'It was difficult at first: the people who'd never shut up in the workshop were suddenly struck dumb! But we persevered, gave it time and now it's come good – everyone feels our meetings are really useful.'**
>
> *Shift Engineer*

Taking time to develop and guide your staff

If leaders don't have much time for people and regard them as so many numbers on the organisational payroll, they are unwilling to devote time to the development and guidance of their staff.

You, however, as a liberating leader, will believe very strongly in giving time to people. You will take time and spend it for the benefit of others, by developing and guiding staff. Since the extent and scale of development required will always depend upon individual or team needs, the amount of time which you will have to devote to it can vary widely. It is one of the hallmarks of the liberating leader that you will give time readily and freely, without counting the hours.

'I can't say "my door is always open", because I haven't got a door – my desk is with everybody else's!'

IT Manager

From time to time, you may find that there are special needs or periods of heavy demand for development. In these circumstances you might enlist the help of others to assist with people development, but it will still be you, as the liberating leader, who makes the arrangements and retains the responsibility.

Dealing effectively with breaches in standards of behaviour

A no-nonsense leadership style deals with breaches in standards of behaviour by making it clear throughout the organisation that transgressions will be subject to summary justice. You, as a liberating leader, will have a different approach. Whilst you believe equally strongly that adherence to standards of behaviour is of paramount importance and that everything must be done to maintain discipline and good order within the organisation, you will achieve those ends by alternative means.

You will see development as the key to improved behaviour, having observed that breaches in standards still occur in the harshest of regimes, despite the tough sanctions. In a liberating atmosphere, however, people improve their standards of behaviour themselves, as a natural consequence of their sense of increased development and enhanced personal responsibility.

There is also a strong link between improved standards of behaviour and the introduction and use of teamworking. Peer pressure is a very strong and effective sanction, and ensures that anyone who breaches the agreed standards learns to improve very quickly.

Treating other people's mistakes as learning opportunities
For some managers and leaders, dealing with mistakes is a straightforward matter: mistakes represent wrongdoing and should be penalised, so that the people concerned do not make them again. Why people make mistakes and whether – if such reasons could be examined – people might be helped to stop making them, is not considered.

As a liberating leader, on the other hand, it is your belief that mistakes can be turned to advantage because people can learn from them. If, when a mistake is made, a frank discussion is held with the person concerned to examine the reasons, the organisation will benefit. Such discussions often reveal that the person who made the mistake has a need. That need may be for specific training or more general development, or for help in handling the workload, or it may simply be for clarification or increased understanding. In any event, whatever the requirement, by treating a mistake as a learning opportunity, additional development takes place.

> **'If somebody drops a clanger, I don't jump on them – I sit down with them and work out what will be better next time.'**
>
> *Production Manager*

The cumulative effect of such a positive attitude towards mistakes is that the organisation becomes increasingly developed and more mature. This helps to foster a healthy spirit of risk-taking, a culture of innovation and the eager acceptance of individual responsibilities.

Your attributes, skills and competencies

The six behaviours which characterise D FOR DEVELOPS PEOPLE AND TEAMS are underpinned by particular attributes, skills or competencies which you, as a liberating leader, will need to use. In particular, we feature two of these, which you may need to extend or develop: **teamworking and teambuilding skills** and **coaching skills**.

Teamworking and teambuilding: tips for liberating leaders

When you are involved in building and developing a team, you need to be aware of the following four different stages in team development:

FORMING	STORMING	NORMING	PERFORMING

Stage 1: forming

You will find that when a team is forming, its members tend to explore, in a very cautious way, the boundaries of acceptable group behaviour. This can often be a testing time for you as a leader and for your authority.

The kinds of forming behaviours you will notice include:

● attempts to define the task and decide how it will be accomplished
● attempts to determine acceptable group behaviour
● attempts to determine how to deal with problems
● decisions on the information to be gathered to solve a problem
● abstract discussions of concepts and issues, and for some, impatience with such discussions and a desire to get on with the task in hand
● discussions of symptoms or problems not relevant to the task in hand
● difficulty in identifying relevant problems
● complaints about the organisation and barriers to the task in hand.

Stage 2: storming

The next stage is the most difficult one for the team. You will notice that they begin to realise the task is probably more difficult than they imagined. They will often become testy, impatient, blameful or over-zealous, arguing about just what action they ought to take.

The kinds of storming behaviours you will observe include:

- arguing amongst themselves, even when actually agreeing on the real issues
- defensiveness and competition between team members
- the emergence of factions and 'taking sides'
- questioning everything: 'why should we do it this way?'
- establishing unrealistic goals
- concerns about excessive work
- a perceived 'pecking order', leading to disunity, tension and jealousy.

Your job as a liberating leader should be to shield the team from the many pressures, directing team energies into making progress towards the goal. When you achieve this, you will find that members of the team are starting to understand one another.

Stage 3: norming

During this stage, members start to reconcile competing loyalties and responsibilities. You will find that they accept the team, acknowledge the ground rules, adjust to their roles in the team and accommodate the individuality of their fellow team members.

The kinds of norming behaviours you will encounter include:

- an attempt to achieve harmony by avoiding conflict
- more friendliness, confiding and a sharing of personal problems
- better discussions and the development of effective team dynamics
- a sense of team cohesion, with a common spirit and goals
- the establishment and maintenance of team ground rules and boundaries
- clearly defined roles
- the establishment of a framework of formal and informal communication.

You will see that as team members begin to work out their differences, they have more time and energy to spend on the project or the task in hand. This stage will show a significant improvement in progress.

Stage 4: performing

By this time the team has settled its relationships and expectations. You will observe that they begin to perform, diagnose and solve problems, choose and implement changes. Team members have discovered each other's strengths and weaknesses and use these to the advantage of all. Thus more productivity is derived from the team than from the individuals.

The kinds of performing behaviours you will detect include:

- humour, used in a constructive way to progress the task
- constructive self-change
- the ability to prevent team problems or work through them
- a close attachment to the team
- accepting responsibility for themselves and for the team's achievement.

By Stage 4, you will find that the team has become an effective, cohesive unit.

So what is this team that has been created through four agonising stages? What actually *is* a team? A useful definition for you is that a team is a group of people with different skills and abilities communicating effectively with each other and working together to achieve clearly identified goals. Although it is possible to 'go it alone' the extent of achievement is limited when people do not work together. One person can have brilliant ideas but may lack the imagination, objectivity or determination to capitalise on them.

In teambuilding you should value the mix of different people with different abilities and skills because, whilst they may be more difficult to mould into a team, ultimately they will prove more creative, responsive and effective.

We develop and build teams because they

- achieve more than the sum of their individual parts
- provide support and help to their members
- generate commitment
- solve problems
- provide learning opportunities
- provide a satisfying, stimulating and enjoyable working environment
- provide organisations with a 'competitive edge'

You may think that you have a team or teams in existence already, but you must be aware of the crucial differences between a real team and a group. People may believe that they belong to a coherent team, but in reality it is merely a loose grouping. There are many, many differences between a group and a team, and they apply to all the following aspects of their activities:

Dependence

In a group, members work independently, sometimes at cross purposes with each other, and may not understand why they are in the group anyway. In a team, however, members recognise their interdependence, understand goals, give mutual support and don't seek personal gain.

Ownership

In a group, the members are not involved in planning and tend to approach their jobs as hired hands. In a team, the members feel a sense of ownership and are committed to goals they themselves helped to establish.

Contribution

In a group, the members are told what to do and are not necessarily encouraged to give ideas and suggestions. Team members, however, contribute to success by using their knowledge and talents and are keen to see the objectives of the team achieved.

Climate

In a group, the members may distrust the motives of others, failing to understand their roles and often displaying divisive opinions. In a team, the members work in a climate of trust, are encouraged to express ideas and opinions openly and welcome questions.

Communication

In a group, members are cautious about what they say, are not interested in the fostering of real understanding, indulge in 'game playing' and set communication traps for the unwary. In a team, however, members practise open and honest communication, make efforts to understand each other's point of view and contribute positively to team meetings.

Training
In a group, members are given limited opportunity to apply new skills and are dominated by a supervisor. In a team, the members are encouraged to develop new skills and are given support by the team and the team leader.

Involvement
In a group, the members are not involved in decision-taking and are left to resolve their own conflict problems. In a team, members are involved in decision-taking and accept decisions, working as a team to resolve conflict.

As a liberating leader, you will want to promote positive teamwork. Here are some actions you can use to help you, arranged in order of increasing team maturity. Under each of the headings, the last item should be brought into play only when your team has become strong and self-confident.

Team goals
● Remind people of team objectives and discuss team performance
● Agree a weekly or a monthly team challenge
● Get the team to devise a mission statement
● Get the team to set its own goals

Openness
● Promote openness by admitting your own mistakes
● Encourage learning by inviting team members to share their mistakes
● Promote self-criticism and peer evaluation

Selection and induction
● Bear in mind the need for a balance of doers, thinkers and carers
● Arrange a systematic planned induction

- Get team members to meet candidates and listen to and act on the feedback
- Discuss induction of new members at team meetings
- Get team members to carry out the induction
- Celebrate the arrival of a new team member
- Say farewell properly to a departing team member

Training
- Arrange team training sessions
- Coach team members
- Promote cross-training of and by team members
- Promote mentoring and coaching by other team members
- Provide a resource area with a wide range of learning materials

Decision-taking and problem-solving
- Whenever possible ask for the views of team members before taking a decision which will affect them – and actually listen to their suggestions
- Involve the team in solving problems and train them in problem-solving techniques – brainstorming, cause and effect analysis and related methods
- When feasible allow the team to take a decision by reaching consensus

Giving feedback on individual performance
- Clarify excellent and minimum performance levels: then give praise when it is earned
- Conduct constructive appraisals and performance reviews and discuss how the individual relates with other team members
- Invite upward appraisals
- Establish team appraisals of each other

Recognising team achievement
- Praise and congratulate success at team meetings
- Be a public relations person for the team and ensure others know of the team's achievements
- Find imaginative ways of celebrating together
- Involve partners in celebrations

In addition to these actions, you should study, and learn from, other successful teams; become a role model for your team by your own personal example; deal promptly and effectively with any potentially destructive conflict between team members (remember they don't have to love each other but they do need to depend on each other); and keep numbers small enough (ideally eight to twelve) to prevent sub-groups forming and fragmenting the whole team.

✓ **Teamworking and teambuilding checklist**

- Remember the four stages of teambuilding
- Be aware of the essential differences between a team and a group
- Always promote positive teamworking as part of your liberating actions
- Discuss, encourage and promote the setting of team goals
- Promote and encourage openness within teams
- Encourage teams to take appropriate responsibility for the selection and induction of new team members
- Organise and promote training, mentoring and coaching of team members
- Involve team members fully in decision-making and problem-solving
- Foster and encourage constructive feedback on performances
- Recognise and celebrate all team achievements
- Study and learn from successful teams

Coaching: tips for liberating leaders

Coaching is not *teaching*. Coaching is not *training*. Coaching is not *instructing*. Coaching is helping people to learn, rather than teaching them. Coaching is assisting people to acquire skills, rather than training them. Coaching is aiding people in their pursuit of knowledge, rather than instructing them.

The essence of coaching is encapsulated in this simple definition:

'Facilitating another person to develop their performance through their own discovery and learning.'

If you aspire to becoming a liberating leader, you need to be effective as a coach. To be effective, you will need to have or to develop the following skills:

- questioning
- reflecting back
- summarising
- generating feedback
- awareness and understanding of body language
- using a 'tentative tone' to reply
- listening to understand – but not to reply
- using silence effectively.

These skills should be used in the belief that people, given the right encouragement and a good listening ear, will find the answers for themselves.

A coaching session makes extensive use of questions to raise awareness and develop responsiveness. These questions, which facilitate the process of self-discovery and self-development, can be grouped under four headings which form a convenient structure and are generally given the slogan **GROW**.

identifying	your	**GOALS**	(long-term and short-term)
	the	**REALITY**	of the current situation
	your	**OPTIONS**	and alternative strategies
	what	**WILL**	you do?

You will find it useful to refer to the section on the use of questions in 'communication tips' in Chapter Four (page 51).

The kinds of questions you need to be able to ask are:

GOALS
- What do you want to achieve from this session?
- Is it realistic?

- How will you recognise that you are performing better?
- Is it challenging?
- Can you measure it?
- Where are you now (say on a scale of one to ten)?
- Where do you want to be?
- What is the timescale within which you could achieve it?
- Are shorter-term goals needed before you target the ultimate goal?
- What would you like to achieve by ...? (naming a date)

REALITY
- What is happening now?
- What have you done about it so far?
- How do you handle ...?
- Is there a particular issue?
- How often?
- Who?
- By whom?

(You should avoid the question 'why', because it often elicits a defensive response; unlike 'what' and 'how' questions, which can allow the other person to explore issues rather than simply justifying their thoughts.)

OPTIONS
- What options do you have?
- What else could you do?
- What is causing you concern?
- Suppose anything was possible?
- What if that obstacle did not exist?
- What sources of help and support do you have?
- What are the costs of your various options?

WILL
- What is your preferred option?
- Do you want to try several or focus on one only?
- Which one would you like to try?

- Are you willing to try that?
- Will that help you achieve your goal?
- What sorts of obstacles would you face?
- How will you overcome them?
- What support do you need?
- When would you want to start?

Use this simple questioning structure to develop your coaching expertise. You will need to practise. Try it out on friends first, if you want. You probably think that you won't know what sorts of questions to ask – but you'll find that you will.

Keep the GROW structure in mind, but don't prepare any kind of script or set of pre-prepared questions. That would be disastrous! If you listen to the person you are coaching and follow their body language and non-verbal messages, you'll find that they themselves give you a lead and indicate the direction in which to go. It may sound a bit strange, but they will prompt you!

It may not be smooth and straightforward at first, but if you practise and persevere you will be surprised how quickly you develop your skills and how soon you start to feel comfortable.

It is important to remember that coaching is concerned with the enhancement of a person's performance at work. It may involve helping the other person to seek their own solutions to personal difficulties and emotions that affect their performance, but do not stray over the line into counselling and therapy, which requires particular expertise and qualifications.

✔ Coaching checklist

- Get clear in your own mind what coaching should really be
- Remember that your aim is to help the other person to develop their performance through their own discovery and learning
- Be aware of all the skills you will need to become a good coach
- If you think that you need to develop some of the qualities further, take action at once

Coaching checklist cont'd

- Become familiar with the **GROW** slogan as the basis for useful questions
- Practise the kinds of questions you can use to identify **goals**
- Practise the kinds of questions you can use to examine the **reality** of the current situation
- Practise the kinds of questions you can use to explore **options** and alternative strategies
- Practise the kinds of questions you can use to determine what the other person **will** do
- Develop your questioning technique until you are comfortable with it
- Keep the structure in mind, but use the other person's responses to move forward in the conversation
- Use questions to raise awareness and develop responsibility in the other person
- Remember to stay with coaching – don't cross the line into counselling

---

D = DEVELOPS PEOPLE AND TEAMS

LIBERATING LEADER BEHAVIOURS

Encourages other people to learn

Encourages people to work together as a team

Regularly meets with the team, as a whole, to review progress

Takes time to develop and guide their staff

Deals effectively with breaches in standards of behaviour

Treats other people's mistakes as learning opportunities

LIBERATING LEADER ATTRIBUTES

A belief that people can learn

A belief that unacceptable behaviour must be dealt with firmly but properly

A belief that teamworking is the most effective way of achieving results

A belief that mistakes are a symptom, not a cause

Encourages others

Seeks learning opportunities

LIBERATING LEADER SKILLS AND COMPETENCIES

Reviewing skills

Effective guidance of others

Effective development of others

Effective participant in disciplinary procedures

TEAMWORKING AND TEAMBUILDING SKILLS

COACHING SKILLS

CHAPTER 7

E means 'example-setting'

The fifth letter of our slogan LEADER gives us another 'E'. This time it is 'E' for EXAMPLE-SETTING. The fifth characteristic of the liberating leader is that he or she has to *provide an example to others*.

Enthusiasm is infectious. Leaders gain respect and commitment by providing a positive and enthusiastic role model. Liberating leaders reinforce the team and organisational values by and through their own behaviour.

If a leader has to take a stand on a matter of principle, this can be a further instance of example-setting to colleagues. The leader in any walk of life (management, politics, religion or the services) who says one thing and then does another is regarded, rightly, as hypocritical. Liberating leaders must always 'practise what they preach'.

The profile of 'example-setting'

If YOU are going to become a liberating leader, then you need to make sure that you can SET AN EXAMPLE. This means, as the LEADER Profile indicates:

- actively encouraging feedback on your own performance
- communicating an air of enthusiasm
- working on your own learning

- practising what you preach
- openly admitting your mistakes
- setting a good example to others by your own behaviour.

Actively encouraging feedback on your own performance

Managerial leaders who use a traditional style tend to feel that if they encourage comments about their own performance their authority will be undermined. Most people working within that kind of regime learn to keep private thoughts about leadership performance to themselves. As a liberating leader, however, you must take the opposite view. By encouraging the non-leaders in your organisation to give you feedback on your performance, you will help to strengthen your leadership, not weaken it.

Setting an example is an integral part of any comprehensive arrangement for liberating leadership, and everyone involved in a leadership role, at whatever level in the organisation, should provide a behavioural model for others to follow.

> **'I'm on the lookout for feedback from everybody, because everybody has something to offer.'**
>
> *Chief Executive, District Council*

This all-embracing model of behaviour calls for the provision of constructive feedback on performance – and that includes leadership performance. There must be no question of an exclusion zone in a liberated organisation!

Communicating an air of enthusiasm

You should recognise that enthusiasm is infectious and that there is a strong case for spreading that kind of infection throughout the organisation! You will be seen as an open, honest and people-oriented leader who knows that visible enthusiasm helps with the liberating process.

> **'Whenever our boss comes round, we all get a bit of a lift – she's so full of it! She bubbles over with enthusiasm about everything!'**
>
> *Office Supervisor*

You will know that initial enthusiasm for the concept of liberation helps to get things started and then a continuing enthusiasm keeps it on the right path of development. It is only by being enthusiastic and, more importantly, being seen to be enthusiastic, that you can ensure the creation of a truly liberating climate.

Working on your own learning
Managerial leaders of the traditional style tend to cultivate an image of strength and infallibility, and so to be seen as 'still learning' goes against the grain. You, however, as a liberating leader, will continue to work hard at your own learning and will have no qualms about revealing this to others. This is another example of how a potential weakness can be turned into a strength – if the leader is continuing to learn, others will surely follow their lead.

> **'I keep a little notebook and every Friday I jot down what I've learned that week. I shall keep it going, even though I retire in four years.'**

> *Chief Executive*

'You learn something new every day' is a frequently heard expression in managerial circles; sadly, nowadays, it is often accompanied by an ironic twist. You, however, as the liberating leader, should rescue it from its fate, resume its straightforward use and commend it to everyone as a daily motto. A particular priority for many managers is to keep abreast of new technology. Pressure to do so is often severe in those organisations which are filled with young, dynamic members of staff who seem to have vast knowledge at their fingertips.

Practising what you preach
One of the complaints which can be made against managerial leaders is that they do not practise what they preach. Orders are issued, rules of working are formulated and behaviours are ordained – but non-leaders may perceive that such arrangements are flouted by the very people who established them. In many cases such allegations are wrong, but organisational mud tends to stick.

As a liberating leader who believes in E FOR EXAMPLE-SETTING, you will not be handicapped in this way, because you believe in organisational democracy and are wedded to the idea that everyone can make a contribution to the organisation. In line with this, it is vital that anyone who has to do any 'preaching' (and though that is not quite the right word, liberating leaders have to expound on certain matters from time to time) should practise what they preach.

Openly admitting your mistakes

You should be ready to admit your mistakes. You should explain the context and the background and then explain the reasons why the mistake was made.

> **'Any manager who says he never makes a mistake is a liar.'**
>
> *Personnel Director*

The open admission of mistakes by a leader is yet another aspect of the liberating climate which the leader has created and is seeking to maintain. By 'confessing' in this way you will not be showing weakness but strength – the strength of leadership which encourages others to admit their mistakes and to do something about them in a constructive way.

Make it clear, through your practical example, that everyone in the organisation is in the same position: your honest action will be rewarded with an honest response. Your admissions will 'give permission' for others to admit their mistakes freely.

Setting a good example to others by your own behaviour

As a liberating leader, it is self-evident that you should and will subscribe to a belief in the power of example. Your behaviour must continue to represent the organisational model which should be followed by everyone.

> **'When he said he was giving up his reserved car space and would take pot luck with the rest of us, I said "he won't keep that up" – but he has!'**
>
> *Security Officer*

Your attributes, skills and competencies

The six behaviours which characterise E FOR EXAMPLE-SETTING are underpinned by particular attributes, skills or competencies which you, as a liberating leader, will need to use. The two that are relevant to this chapter, and which you may need to extend or develop, are: **the skills of seeking and receiving feedback** and **self-managed development skills**.

Seeking and receiving feedback: tips for liberating leaders

Seeking and receiving feedback is an essential tool which you need to develop if you are to become an effective practitioner of liberating leadership. You should seek out feedback from your colleagues, from your staff, from customers and indeed from anyone who is in a position to give you information which you can make use of.

You must convince the other party that you have a positive and enlightened attitude towards feedback and that you are in earnest. It is essential to ensure that what you receive from the other party reflects their view of your actions and behaviour accurately and that it will be as useful to you as possible. Emphasise that all feedback is helpful, whether it could be regarded as 'positive' or 'negative'.

Since other people can prove somewhat ineffective at providing feedback, you must ensure that they give you what you want, 'managing' and manipulating their responses so that they give you the right kind of information. Organise them so that they help you.

Make them understand that you want clear, hard information, not soft or vague comments. In particular, you need to emphasise, at least to start with, that you want information and views that you can then use to make your own decisions – you do not want to be told what to do. You may find that this is an unusual concept for many people to grasp, because they *like* telling other people what they ought to do.

You also need to analyse your own approach and possible response. Accepting feedback can represent a problem for most of us: our natural tendency is to reject what other people say to us about our behaviour.

If you think that you have such a tendency, there may be a number of reasons for it. Think about the following:

You try to reject the validity of the information you are being given. You may say to yourself, 'That's not true!', and set your face against it. That would be unwise, particularly if you have sought feedback from the other person. You should accept that it is valid and take account of it.

You question the competence of the person giving you the feedback. If you have asked the other person, very specifically, to give you feedback, it would be perverse, having received it, to turn round and claim that the other party is not competent to supply it. If they were suitable before, they must still be suitable afterwards.

You attribute false motives to the other person. If you fear that the other person may give you feedback which reflects some personal malice towards you, you should not have chosen them in the first place! Think carefully – are your suspicions about them engendered by the nature of the feedback you have received? Remember that honest feedback can be either 'positive' or 'negative', and will remain honest. It doesn't suddenly become false just because you regard it as negative!

You claim that they have drawn attention to behaviour which is not typical. You're clutching at straws now! You're suggesting that, 'Well, yes, what they say is true, but I don't usually do that. I've never done it before and I haven't done it since!' That won't really wash. Once again, you should accept and take account of honest feedback.

You claim that it would be impossible to change in the way implied by the feedback. In effect you are saying: 'I accept what you say, but I'm not prepared to respond and alter things'. This is a way of avoiding doing anything and comes quite close to saying that you don't accept the feedback anyway. You need to learn to review the feedback you receive, not to reject it. You should work on the assumption that honest feedback has been given honestly and you should take it on board. You need to digest it thoroughly and sort out its value.

Since it is highly probable that you will seek and receive feedback on a number of different occasions from a number of different people, you will be able to build up a picture of your own behaviour from a variety of different angles. In that way, feedback which is reinforced will provide you with clear messages to act upon, whilst scattered and contradictory feedback will be discarded.

As the objective is to improve performance, you will be looking for feedback which is related directly to you and to your role in the organisation. General feedback, which is not associated with you and your performance in a specific job, will be virtually useless. Nor do you want casual feedback, imparted on an *ad lib* basis in the middle of a conversation which has another purpose. Feedback must be structured and should be communicated in a purposeful setting.

The supplier of the feedback should give careful thought to it and needs to be aware of your sensitivities and possible reactions. This does not mean that you expect them to alter or dilute their observations in any way: it simply means that they present their findings carefully and professionally. You, in your turn, have to be ready to receive their findings in a calm and professional manner.

✔ Feedback checklist

- Adopt a positive, consistent attitude towards feedback
- Make sure everyone knows that you are seeking feedback
- Spell out openly that you want honest feedback, so that others are clear about what they should provide
- Make it clear to the people who are to supply the feedback that *you want* them to discuss your behaviour and how it is perceived by them
- Make it clear to them that *you do not want* them to tell you what you ought to do
- Think carefully about your own possible responses and the way you might handle feedback
- When you receive feedback about your behaviour in a particular situation, review it carefully and take it into account when comparable situations arise in the future
- Encourage people to give you feedback which relates to your specific role in the organisation, rather than general feedback, which may be of little value
- Use feedback from different people to build up a picture of your behaviour as seen from a variety of angles

Self-managed development: tips for liberating leaders

How much learning have you undertaken as a manager? Perhaps you've attended courses and learning events run by specialised trainers, but you may have less experience of self-managed learning. You'll find that self-managed learning is very different from trainer-led learning, mainly because you have, in part, to act as your own trainer. Professional trainers are experts in the learning process, so you'll need to know more about that to make your personal development effective.

An enlightened approach to management and leadership goes hand in glove with a new approach to personal development. Whilst the traditional formal course, led by a trainer, may still have a place, its pre-eminence has faded. Today, a more comprehensive and flexible approach is in evidence, utilising less formal methods. You, as a liberating leader, should seek an effective combination of informality and practicality by using work itself as the main medium for your further learning and development.

You can devise very effective work-based activities and experiences, supported by the use of appropriate self-study materials and access to electronic learning. Such self-managed personal development is still evolving, and you may require additional expertise. Even though your managerial skills might be second to none, you will have to top up on the skills of learning and personal development.

Personal development

Personal development means the development of the individual person and can cover enhancing existing skills, acquiring new ones, accepting different responsibilities, gaining additional confidence, together with a whole range of processes designed to add breadth, depth and strength to a person's individual capability and competence. Under a liberating umbrella, personal development involves a partnership between the organisation, which has the need and requires the enhanced skills, and the individual who wants to supply those skills.

Effective personal development requires the systematic and comprehensive assessment of individual and corporate needs, followed by the deployment of a variety of development methods and techniques designed to meet those assessed needs.

Self-managed personal development

Self-managed personal development means taking responsibility for your own learning, but you cannot develop yourself single-handedly. You must draw upon all the resources available – peers, bosses, experts, personnel and training specialists, other sections within your organisation, your partners and your friends.

What you need to do

The process will involve you in a number of different activities with which you may not be fully familiar. You will have to:

- set markers for successful performance
- evaluate performance against those markers
- identify learning needs in the light of performance
- identify learning opportunities
- plan learning against the identified needs
- review the learning processes used.

Will you be free to choose the subjects you want to pursue, or will your organisation set the agenda? Any organisation endorsing liberating leadership will be conscious of such conflicting demands and should provide a balanced response, stimulating individual learning in order to satisfy both the needs of the organisation and the aspirations of individuals. The result should be a *developmental partnership* in which both parties have particular responsibilities.

A wide range of different methods and approaches is available to help you with your self-managed development. Reading, studying videos, listening to audiotapes, carrying out projects, undertaking short attachments, learning from job-swaps, shadowing another manager, trying role reversal: all these and many more can be used.

The methods available include both the formal and the informal. The learning provision may be either formal and structured or informal and loosely organised. The process used by the individual may have different degrees of formality and structure.

Formal, trainer-led courses and learning programmes are normally specific customised activities established solely for learning purposes.

Informal self-development, on the other hand, involves the use of regular, everyday activities adopted for learning purposes. Such activities have a prime purpose which is managerial, but a developmental function can be built in.

Work-based self-development means using the ongoing work situation and exploiting any *ad hoc* learning opportunities which occur. Self-development opportunities can also occur externally, in the 'non-work' environment: you may find that activities undertaken in your leisure and relaxation time are beneficial to your development and can have a learning content.

A great many books, videos and audiotapes are available and suitable for self-study. Such materials are comfortably familiar, readily obtainable and relatively inexpensive. Because these learning materials are fully compatible with the traditional managerial office environment, they are often still preferred. Developments in information technology, however, mean that very sophisticated learning packages are now available, both to organisations and to individuals.

You should take a good look at what's available and choose the learning methods you feel most comfortable with. Remember, however, that you don't have to select just one method – you can try several different ones if you like.

When pursuing your own self-managed development, do not be inhibited by any of the materials or approaches you choose. You are beholden to no one and are quite free to change! Adjust and modify what you do in the light of experience. It is vital that you should feel comfortable with every learning activity you undertake: if you do not, you will not learn very much.

Self-managed development gives you the freedom to pursue just what you want and to feel responsible and accountable: it epitomises the liberating leadership approach. You should beware, however, of becoming too inward-looking. Don't load your shoulders with everything, otherwise you'll soon feel that development is a very lonely business. You'll find it helps if you talk to other people and consult them about what you're doing. You may need help and advice. If you do, ask. Confide in others, tell them about your experiences and build up your personal support network. The people in your network will be aware of what you're trying to achieve and will empathise with you. Enlist their support and ask them for feedback.

Support networks of this kind are a feature of an open organisation which has embraced liberating leadership. The fact that you yourself are still learning and are managing your own development will exemplify much of what 'liberating' really means.

✓ **Self-managed development checklist**

- Be aware of new approaches to learning and development
- Think through your own development needs
- Make a plan to meet your development needs and think about how you're going to manage that plan
- Review the various learning processes available and decide which ones you're going to use and how
- Plan any work-based development activities and experiences
- Plan any solo development exercises you intend to use
- Plan your use of any self-study materials and packages
- Talk to your colleagues and think about a suitable support network
- Ask for help and feedback as and when you need it

E = EXAMPLE TO OTHERS

LIBERATING LEADER BEHAVIOURS

Actively encourages feedback on their own performance

Communicates an air of enthusiasm

Works on their own learning

Practises what they preach

Openly admits mistakes

Sets a good example to others by their own behaviour

LIBERATING LEADER ATTRIBUTES

A belief that it is important to set a good example

A belief that one should welcome feedback from others

A belief that it is important to admit own mistakes

Is visibly enthusiastic

Has a sharing approach

Always ready to learn

Consistent – doesn't say one thing and do another

LIBERATING LEADER SKILLS AND COMPETENCIES

One-to-one skills

Able to admit and learn from mistakes

Aware of effect of own behaviour upon others

SKILLS OF SEEKING AND RECEIVING FEEDBACK

SELF-MANAGED DEVELOPMENT SKILLS

CHAPTER 8

R means 'relationship-building through trust'

Our final letter in the slogan LEADER gives us an 'R'. It is 'R' for RELATIONSHIP-BUILDING THROUGH TRUST. This sixth characteristic of the liberating leader is that he or she has to *build relationships through trust* by means of his or her own behaviour.

Staff must be able to trust their leaders. Trust, however, cannot be demanded – it must be earned. Research confirms that the key to trust lies in the belief system of the leader, which, as outlined in Chapter One, comprises self-belief, belief in, and beliefs about, others, and a belief in fairness.

Staff should be able to trust their manager or leader to take decisions which will ensure the success of the team, section, department or organisation. The leader's track record of results and how they have been achieved is therefore important. Despite a good track record, however, people will not have confidence in a person who does not appear to have confidence in themselves. Leaders must demonstrate their self-belief by their daily behaviour. It is particularly important to be unruffled when under pressure. Staff are unlikely to trust a leader who is seen to panic in a crisis.

Leaders will soon lose trust if they knowingly mislead or lie. The discovery that someone has been deceitful casts doubt over everything they do. Honesty does not necessarily require full disclosure. It does, however, require a clear explanation of when complete candour should not be expected, and why it is not appropriate.

Integrity involves passing on the credit for the work of someone else – not taking it. Personal interest must not be put before the interests of others.

Fairness requires us to be even-handed in our dealings with staff. It precludes having favourites who receive special treatment and discriminating against individuals or groups of people. Leaders should avoid bias by listening to every viewpoint and collecting all the facts before making decisions.

Because trust is mutual, people are unlikely to trust a manager or leader who clearly does not trust them. Liberating leaders see the good in others and give people the benefit of the doubt, without being naive. They genuinely want others to succeed. Over the years bureaucratic systems and procedures have evolved within many organisations based on the assumption that people cannot be trusted. Liberating leaders challenge and change these systems.

The profile of relationship-building through trust

If YOU are going to become a liberating leader, then you need to make sure that you can BUILD RELATIONSHIPS and that you can do so THROUGH TRUST. This means, as the LEADER Profile indicates:

- not putting self-interest before the interests of your staff
- keeping promises and doing what you say you will do
- being in touch with, and sensitive to, other people's feelings
- being calm in a crisis, and when under pressure
- being honest and truthful
- not taking personal credit for other people's work
- always being fair.

We see from an examination of the list that the behaviours in this final segment of LEADER are manifestations of innate personal beliefs rather than learned behaviours. For example, 'being honest and truthful' are personal characteristics based on beliefs. At the same time, however, that underlying honesty and truthfulness will be reflected through the particular actions and behaviours. So, for 'being honest and truthful' we could substitute 'acting in an honest and truthful way'.

Not putting self-interest before the interests of your staff

A liberating climate encourages everyone to put selfishness behind them. In developing and sustaining a genuinely selfless atmosphere, a special responsibility falls upon the leadership: it is imperative that people like yourself, who are in that role, should not put your own self-interest before the interests of others. Moreover, there should not be the slightest suspicion that you might be doing so. Collectively, the liberating leadership must find ways to make it clear to the rest of the staff that the team comes first.

> **'I've seen a few come and go – most of them would sell their own grandmother. This one's different, though – he really looks after our interests.'**
>
> *Laboratory Technician*

Keeping promises and doing what you say you will do

Under a liberating leadership, the climate is an open, flexible and enquiring one in which, somewhat paradoxically, leaders such as yourself can come under more pressure. Because of the democratic atmosphere, you will be asked to make more promises and to do more for others. As a consequence, you might feel tempted to promise more readily and then find that you cannot deliver.

You must ensure that you are able to keep every promise that you make. Liberating leaders should in some ways be more cautious about making promises and public statements. You must be completely certain that a promise can be met before it is made, otherwise that promise will come back to haunt you.

Being in touch with, and sensitive to, other people's feelings

The liberating leader cannot create a suitable climate and atmosphere in his or her organisation without being in touch with, and sensitive to, other people's feelings. The feelings of others, and their response to what is being developed, are crucial to the successful establishment of a properly open and democratic organisation. It can only be maintained in operation, begin to prosper and meet the needs of the organisation through a continued observance of the sensitivities of others. If you ignore the feelings of others, you could begin to encounter some unwanted 'us and them' problems.

> **'I saw the system demonstrated at the NEC and I wanted to buy it there and then. But then I thought, "If I was an operator, how would I feel about that?" – so I didn't.'**
>
> *Managing Director, Garment Manufacture*

Being calm in a crisis, and when under pressure

As a liberating leader, you must recognise the importance of remaining calm in a crisis. It is important not only for your personal needs but also because of the special position which you hold. By remaining calm, you can exert a calming influence on the section, team or department and the individuals within it.

This characteristic is particularly important when leadership is spread throughout the organisation. Each small leadership 'station' can help to cope with pressure by remaining cool, calm and collected. In this way the liberated organisation stays on an even keel.

> **'When there's a crisis, other managers run around like headless chickens, but she's as cool as a cucumber. She uses the energy she saves for thinking.'**
>
> *Packing Supervisor*

Being honest and truthful

It should not be necessary to specify that a leader should be honest and truthful, but you will know that in the past certain leaders have been perceived as being somewhat economical with the truth. Liberating leadership, however, provides a climate in which everyone can work openly and collaboratively in pursuit of the interests of the organisation as a whole. For this climate to be effective, all the internal dealings and interactions between individuals and groups should be honest and the truth must be the common currency of the organisation.

Not taking personal credit for other people's work

Under liberating leadership, all those who contribute to the work of an organisation can collaborate to achieve that vital competitive edge. The establishment of a sensible 'all for one and one for all' atmosphere helps to eliminate the kinds of internal competition and petty jealousies which can be so damaging and counter-productive, instead freeing up individuals to achieve their full potential at every level.

The new climate requires everyone to contribute and to receive credit for what they do. Nobody can take credit for anyone else's success, least of all anyone in a leadership position. You will build relationships by giving a lead to others and by developing a climate of trust. Taking personal credit for something which rightly belongs to someone else would prevent trust-building and destroy any partially built relationships.

Always being fair

Anyone in any managerial position should always show fairness. In an ideal world there would never be any unfairness: everyone would treat each other with scrupulous fair-mindedness.

Reality is different. In the hectic and uncertain world of work, with rapid decision-making, turnover of personnel and the ever-present threat of change, unfair actions and attitudes are perhaps understandable.

> **'The gaffer's always been very fair with me. He doesn't jump to conclusions: he gets all the facts first. Then he tells it to you straight, which is fair enough, even when you're in the hot seat.'**
>
> *HGV Driver*

Liberating leadership, however, has to be fair leadership. It cannot afford to be otherwise. It should be built on the six segments of LEADER and, as we know, the vital last piece in the jigsaw is 'relationships'. Proper and effective relationships can only be built up if there is consistent fairness. It is up to the leader to encourage it, to show it and to live it.

Your attributes, skills and competencies

The seven behaviours which characterise R FOR RELATIONSHIPS BUILT ON TRUST are underpinned by particular attributes, skills or competencies which you, as a liberating leader, will need to use. This chapter ends with an examination of two of these, which you may need to extend or develop. In this case, the need is not so much for skills, as for understanding: **understanding about ethics** and **understanding about values**.

Understanding about ethics: tips for liberating leaders

Ethics involves the philosophical study of the moral values of human conduct and the rules and principles that ought to govern it. By studying both moral and immoral actions, ethics allows society to make well-founded judgements about the acceptability of different behaviours.

Ethics promotes a collection of principles, but these are different from laws. Figure 6 opposite illustrates how ethics goes further than the law and in many cases how the law is 'catching up' with ethics.

Almost everyday we encounter examples of politicians and corporate executives behaving in ways that call into question their honesty, morals and personal code of ethics. Distasteful business practices come to light in many places and investigative journalists feast with relish upon rumours of dishonesty and cheating by company directors.

Ethical standards, whether implicit or explicit, have always played a fundamental role in the management of people. Today ethics is used to bring together disparate issues such as health and safety, commercial practice and environmental factors. It also helps to clarify the thin line between a hard bargain and sharp practice.

Organisational circumstances are always changing and new

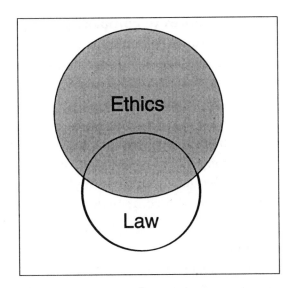

Fig. 6.
Relationship
between ethics and
law

developments produce new ethical issues. Environmental awareness,
technological advance, international influences, changing markets,
legislation, public enquiries, new employment patterns and greater career
mobility can all force organisations to re-evaluate their ethical policies.
When an organisation begins to practise liberating leadership, it abandons
hierarchical structures and introduces devolved decision-making. This
increase in the number of centres of decision-making makes it imperative
that the organisation has an agreed code of ethics and that all decisions
should be properly tested against it.

As a liberating leader, you ought to be aware at all times of the
ethical implications and consequences of the decisions that you are
called upon to make. You will find it helpful to ask yourself the
following questions when you attempt to measure the ethical quality
of your decision-making:

Is it legal?

Does your decision break any local, national or international law? You
should consider this question not only in terms of the letter of the law
but also its spirit and intention. You should ensure that the decision is such
that there is no possibility of discrimination occurring against anybody.

Does it conform to company policy?

Many companies demonstrate their concern about ethical issues by publishing and displaying statements of policy on ethical matters. If your organisation has such a policy statement and you make a decision that contravenes it in some way, it is probable that your decision is unethical. We use the word 'probable' to emphasise that uncertainties and questions of interpretation might mean that you are not necessarily in the wrong. You may take a decision in good faith and subsequently find that, because your company's policy statement is ambiguous or badly phrased, you come under fire.

Is it fair?

If you are to maintain good long-term relationships with colleagues, suppliers and customers, it is important that your dealings with them are fair and properly balanced. Both sides should feel that they are gaining from the relationship and want it to continue. For example, you could, as a leader in a large organisation, use muscle to threaten and browbeat a small trader. It might be legal and it might be within company policy, but it would not be fair.

Can I face myself and my family?

You will find that this is a key question and the one which you use to decide ultimately whether or not something is ethical. How would you feel if you found that your decision had been published in a national newspaper? How would you feel if it had been featured in a television consumer affairs programme? How would you feel if your children were taunted with it in the school playground?

The immediacy of these possibilities, and the wide opportunities for mischief-making that they represent, emphasises the fact that this question is probably the most powerful of the four in terms of helping you to make decisions which could have ethical implications.

As you face ethical dilemmas in your decision-making, you will draw upon your own personal ethics as well as any company policy statements. Use the following ethical decision-making process to assist you in coming to the right decision:

1. Recognise and clarify the dilemma.
2. Get all the possible facts.
3. List your options – all of them (bearing in mind that in every scenario, there are at least two alternatives).
4. Test each option by asking:
   - Is it legal?
   - Does it conform to company policy?
   - Is it fair?
   - Is it right?
   - Will it be beneficial?
5. Make your decision.
6. Double-check your decision by asking:
   - How would I feel if my family found out about this?
   - How would I feel if my decision was published in a newspaper?
7. Take action.

Some ethical quandaries

In your working life within a business organisation, you, as a liberating leader, will encounter a substantial number of ethical quandaries. You may come across these in your dealings with suppliers, customers, local authorities or within various sections or departments of your own organisation. The following list is just a selection:

- Greed
- Cover-ups and misrepresentation in reporting and control procedures
- Misleading product or service claims
- Reneging or cheating on negotiated terms
- Establishing policy that is likely to cause others to lie to get the job done
- Disloyalty to the company as soon as times get rough
- Poor product quality
- Humiliating people at work or by stereotypes in advertising
- Favouritism
- Price-fixing
- Sacrificing the innocent and helpless in order to get things done

- Suppression of freedom of speech, choice, or personal relationships
- Failing to speak up when unethical practices occur
- Making a product decision that perpetrates a questionable safety issue
- Knowingly exaggerating the advantages of a plan in order to get needed support
- Failing to address areas of bigotry, sexism, or racism
- Climbing the corporate ladder by stepping on others
- Promoting the destructive go-getter instead of the competent co-operator
- Refusing to work properly with other areas of the company
- Not taking responsibility for injurious practices
- Abusing corporate perks.

You will have to face up to such quandaries on a regular basis. A liberating organisation is also an ethical organisation and it cannot hide from its responsibility to behave ethically. You will have to take each case as you encounter it and check it through, using the decision-making process suggested.

Understanding about values: tips for liberating leaders

'Values' are defined in The Collins English Dictionary as *the moral principles and beliefs or accepted standards of a person or social group*. Clearly, we are standing here on similar ground to that occupied by ethics.

As you know, the behaviour of the liberating leader is strongly influenced by certain basic beliefs – self-belief, belief in, and beliefs about, others, and a belief in fairness. These become, in effect, accepted standards, coupled with other standards which should influence his or her managerial behaviour.

Organisational values

Many organisations nowadays have established a set of corporate values, which they publish internally and externally. It may well cover issues such as the corporate attitude towards employees, customers and suppliers and the corporate policies on, say, quality and safety.

You, as a liberating leader working within a specific organisation, should have your own values, which you may discover are not necessarily aligned exactly with those of your employer. It is important, however, that you do not dilute or compromise your own personal values, which should be genuine and properly thought out and always consistent with your liberating leadership beliefs.

Individual organisations should always draw up their own statement of corporate values, preferably after consulting as widely as possible amongst managers and staff. If you are involved in this, try to ensure that the resulting document is genuine and original, not just a revamping of a statement which someone has borrowed from another company. You should also encourage your teams to prepare and establish their own statements of values, taking account of individual and corporate statements.

R for RELATIONSHIPS BUILT ON TRUST

LIBERATING LEADER BEHAVIOURS

Does not put self-interest before interests of their staff
Keeps promises and does what they say they will do
Is in touch with, and sensitive to, people's feelings
Is calm in a crisis, and when under pressure
Is honest and truthful
Does not take personal credit for other people's work
Is always fair

LIBERATING LEADER ATTRIBUTES

A belief in the importance of honesty and truthfulness
A belief that promises should be kept
A belief that one's own interests should not be put before
those of others
Sensitivity to the feelings of others
Remaining calm under pressure
Honesty and truthfulness
Gives others credit for their achievements
Fairness

LIBERATING LEADER SKILLS AND UNDERSTANDING

Interpersonal skills

ETHICS
VALUES

Liberating leadership action portrait no. 1: the Logistics Department of Astra Charnwood

The next four chapters describe liberating leadership in action, providing examples of companies and organisations which have adopted liberating principles and applied them to their own situation in various ways. The first one affords a striking example of how liberating leadership can create a positive and empowered climate which gives rise to substantial benefits. The organisation concerned is the Logistics Department of Astra Charnwood.

The organisation

The visitor who has come to talk about liberating leadership and empowerment is greeted with, 'Empowerment? We've empowered everybody here, including the cleaners!'

The Logistics Department serves the whole of the large Astra complex located on the outskirts of Loughborough. One thousand people work on the site, which means, in the words of the Department's Logistics Manager: 'We have 1000 customers'.

The Department provides a wide range of services to the site. There are seven distinct functions:

- Postal Services
- Goods Receiving
- Inventory Control
- Distribution
- Bulk Storage
- Waste Management
- Administration.

Until 1996, these different functions were organised and run as segregated sections, with a rigid, multi-level hierarchical structure, involving supervisors, chargehands and shopfloor workers. It was a typical example of a traditional command and control structure, with a place for everyone and everyone knowing their place.

Each person had a detailed job description, which made it very clear what they were expected to do. It also, by implication, made it very clear what they were not expected to do: think ... use their initiative ... make any decisions ... use common sense ... take responsibility ... be accountable.

Reviewing the situation

The Department decided to carry out a review of what it was doing and the way in which it was doing it. Its existing staff were asked a number of searching questions and a survey was conducted amongst the customers throughout the site.

When the replies were analysed it was apparent that, whilst the systems which had been set up to serve customers were sound in themselves, they had one potential weakness – the people who were operating the systems worked in a manner that was too regimented, too rigid and too slow to react. 'It was clear to us', says the Logistics Manager, 'that we had created a natural home for Mister Jobsworth. No one strayed even a millimetre outside their allotted task and everyone waited to be told everything.'

The new structure

As a result of the review, the Logistics Department decided to sweep away the middle layers of management and supervision and adopt the flattest organisational structure it could create. Today it has a Logistics Manager and seven autonomous groups of people working in their specialised fields. These groups, whilst reporting to the Logistics Manager, operate on a day-to-day basis through the newly created post of Coordinator. The Coordinator is not a manager of people but acts as a focus for the rapid exchange of information, provides help and assistance when required and ensures the smooth running of a multifariously tasked operation.

Within each of the workgroups everyone is a specialist in a designated task or group of tasks. In addition, however, he or she also provides backup to another area of work. Thus everyone has a second string to their bow, ensuring that if anyone is unavoidably absent, cover is available. For obvious reasons, this system cannot cope with a flu epidemic, but it can take occasional absences in its stride.

The Manager has now discarded all those long-winded job descriptions. Everyone has a short and simple document which provides a clear indication of what is expected of them. 'If you can't get the job on to half a page of A4, then there must be something wrong!' says the Manager.

The responsibilities

The new documents have eliminated the word 'do' and replaced it with 'responsible for' or 'assist with'. This allows each job-holder the freedom to do the job in their own way, planning the various tasks required and then implementing them over the working day as necessary. 'We've given them responsibility for their own life and their own destiny', explains the Logistics Manager.

An example of this is that the delivery drivers have now been given responsibility for serving their customers. They plan their route, organise the pick-ups and arrange the loading of their van in the most suitable and effective way. It used to be very different: in the past, for example, a driver who got a flat tyre had to get permission to change the wheel! Now the drivers know that they are free to have the repair done as quickly and as conveniently as possible.

Managing the operation

The Logistics Manager finds that he is now able to operate with a very light rein. Describing his managerial style as 'management by walking about', he uses the method regularly, chatting with individuals to make sure that he is in the picture about any problems or potential problems.

As individuals and groups have taken on greater responsibility, there have inevitably been occasions when they have made wrong decisions. Mistakes have been made and the people concerned have realised that. Now the Manager's policy is to wait for the individuals concerned to acknowledge that a mistake has been made and then discuss it, instead of coming down hard on the 'transgressor' in the old way.

Annual performance reviews are now treated in a very different way from previously. Individuals prepare their own reviews and the whole process is no longer confrontational. There is a positive approach to reviewing performance, and the concept of continuous improvement is supported throughout the Division.

Several improvement projects are now underway and certain members of staff who used to look no further than the next salary slip have become interested in building the future of the Department.

Flexibility

The empowered and liberated climate has led to a striking flexibility in the operation of the different workgroups. Whilst each individual has their own specialised role, the 'second string' approach means that genuine, meaningful and well-informed cover is provided when unavoidable absences occur. Thus a delivery driver can work in Postal Services, or someone who is a regular in Waste Management may assist with Inventory Control.

This backup system is an excellent example of the benefits that can accrue when past rigidities are consigned to history. It means that individuals can acquire additional skills, develop greater all-round understanding of the business and offer an enhanced CV when company vacancies occur.

Support

Attempts to create a liberating climate can sometimes fail, if empowerment and increased responsibility are not accompanied by extra managerial support. Effective support is certainly provided at Astra and in many instances it takes a tangible and eminently practical form. 'Real practical support is vital', says the Logistics Manager. 'We have to give them the tools to do the job.' Since the new approach was put into place, there have been several instances of workgroups saying, in effect: 'We could do the job more efficiently if we had ...' Usually, the case is well made and the additional equipment subsequently installed. One example of this practical support has been the introduction of vans with tail-lifts for on-site delivery. Under the previous regime, any drivers who might have suggested such an adaptation were regarded as lazy and potential troublemakers.

Support is also given through the provision of additional training courses and by offering information and knowledge to individuals that will enable them to acquire a greater understanding of their jobs.

Astra Charnwood represents a clear and very practical example of liberating leadership in action in the workplace. A genuine and discernible revolution has been brought about – in attitudes, in responsiveness, in the working atmosphere and in standards of performance.

The LEADER Profile at work

When the LEADER Profile was checked against the kind of leadership exhibited at Astra Charnwood, this is what we found:

L FOR LIBERATES

There exists a definite 'no-blame' culture and those closest to each group of tasks clearly take their own decisions about those tasks.

Full and open communication is obviously encouraged although, interestingly, some staff have said to the Logistics Manager: 'You don't communicate with us as much as you used to!' Apart from indicating that in management you can never win, this observation highlights the difference between quantity and quality. The Manager reckons that in the old days there used to be a lot of 'telling' and one-way communication, whereas nowadays this has been replaced by selective 'asking' and genuine two-way conversations.

With the flat structure and the liberating climate, the multifarious operations undertaken by the Department have to proceed on the basis of trust, not suspicion. This is particularly significant when, because of the nature of the work, hazardous materials are handled and rigorous national standards, both of quality and performance, have to be maintained.

New ideas are clearly encouraged, although the nature of the services provided does reduce the opportunities to propose major change. Finally, there is a minimum of interference by the leadership with the work of individuals.

E FOR ENCOURAGES AND SUPPORTS

The leadership is wedded to the notion that praise pays real dividends: 'We have discovered that public criticisms don' work, but public congratulations do work!'

The problems which individual people might   e are listened to and care is taken to watch for signs of stress. People can be temporarily placed in a role that involves less responsibility to help them overcome the effects of stress, whether job-related or not.

Staff are always supported when they need it and the leadership goes out of its way to show that it has faith in the workforce.

A FOR ACHIEVES PURPOSE

The Logistics Department provides essential services to a busy and complex site where advanced scientific work is undertaken. Results are paramount and all work must be performed not only with a high degree of competence but also to a high standard of accuracy. This means setting and meeting targets and also seeking constantly to improve. 'Continuous Quality Improvement' (CQI) is the slogan, and the liberating climate enables it to progress.

D FOR DEVELOPS PEOPLE AND TEAMS

So far as this section of the profile is concerned, there is less all-round evidence of liberating leadership behaviour, but encouragement is certainly given to enable individuals to work together as a team and for people to keep on learning.

The leadership makes a particular point of dealing with mistakes in an enlightened way. In the event of mistakes, errors of judgement or failure to meet targets, discussions are held in order to identify reasons and causes, so that any repetitions can be eliminated.

E FOR EXAMPLE TO OTHERS

An enthusiastic example is set by the leadership. It is not the frenetic sort of enthusiasm encountered in some organisations; rather, it reflects the calm, well-organised atmosphere which pervades the working areas. It is made clear that everyone in the Department is working to the same agenda, learning together and seeking performance improvements as a unit.

R FOR RELATIONSHIPS BUILT ON TRUST

Relationships built on trust form a very strong part of the profile. The leadership does not put self-interest before the interests of the staff and it keeps its promises. The practice of 'making the walking do the talking' is very much in evidence, so that the Manager remains in close touch with everyone and is sensitive about individual feelings. The good relationships which have been built up and the climate of honesty, fairness and trust are plain for all to see.

Leadership achievements

Astra Charnwood is an excellent example of how liberating leadership can be exercised to good practical effect in an integrated organisation. So far as leadership behaviours are concerned, our review of the LEADER Profile showed that over 80 per cent of the itemised behaviours are strongly in evidence in this organisation.

CHAPTER 10

Liberating leadership action portrait no. 2: Constar International UK Ltd

This portrait illustrates the effectiveness of liberating leadership in a hectic manufacturing environment which provides 'just-in-time' supplies to its many customers. The company is Constar International UK Ltd.

The products

The company manufactures plastic bottles on a large factory site at Sherburn-in-Elmet, in rural Yorkshire. A wide range of types, shapes and sizes is produced, using a two-stage process: first a suitable 'pre-form' is made and then that is blown out to the requisite specification.

The factory also makes the caps and stoppers for bottles and it produces 'own-label' pre-forms for customers who have integrated 'form and fill' bottling plants.

The organisation

There are 250 people employed on site. The organisation chart is simple and flat, with an Operations Director overseeing the four functional areas of sales, production, warehousing and administration.

The production function, headed by a Production Manager, is

divided into four self-contained production areas, each with its own Process Manager. Each Process Manager has a flexible team of operators, fork-lift truck drivers, quality-control people and engineers.

There are four rotating shifts and the plant is in operation seven days a week throughout the year, with individual machines shut down for planned maintenance as appropriate. There are four Shift Managers, each of whom supervises the smooth running of the factory during their rotating duty periods.

The teams

Each area production team is a self-sufficient workgroup. Whilst each team member has a designated role, there is no demarcation and people cover and fill in for one another as necessary. Operators can carry out quality control tasks, fork-lift truck drivers and engineers can operate machines and operators can make simple repairs and adjustments. What people do is determined by the task in hand, not by their notions of status.

Teams use information and evidence to solve problems. A simple manual system of information collection is used and then computers are employed to analyse and process the information. Simple visual displays of trends and situations are available, so that everyone is in continuous contact with the current situation on a particular shift.

There are no team leaders as such: the four area production teams operate as self-managed teams. When a problem or issue arises, there is no question of referring to someone outside the team: rather, it is handled inside, if at all possible.

An inverted pyramid

The factory arrangements provide a very good example of the inverted pyramid type of organisational structure. In a practical sense, it is the area production teams which occupy 'the top', because they represent the plant so far as daily tasks, issues and problems are concerned. Customers with a practical concern do not ring the Operations Director, or the Production Manager or even a Process Manager: they contact the people they know in the area production team, who can normally deal with it.

Of course this does not mean that the aforementioned managers are redundant. Management provides advice, help and support for the team on a continuous basis and at the same time works on problems and issues which are more complex and longer term than those thrown up in daily production. It's really such a simple concept: everyone just takes responsibility for what they can do best.

In former times, the factory was organised on a traditional 'steep pyramid' basis, with lots of messages passing up and down, so inverting and flattening the pyramid required hard work and dedication. A lot of effort has gone into building relationships between the production teams and customers. Constar have trained staff from various customers and the customers in turn have provided information and training for operators and engineers.

In a similar way, the staff of suppliers and the production teams have been brought closer together through mutual knowledge and understanding of issues. When offered the chance to widen their contacts and their responsibilities, production personnel have grasped it eagerly, reaping the benefit in terms of a more interesting and fulfilling life on the production floor.

Flexibility

The area production teams have grown and developed since they were formed and teamworking is now excellent. This did not happen overnight: everyone had to work at it. A great deal of discussion and a lot of learning was needed. Gradually, a more open attitude towards learning developed. In particular, the engineers gradually realised that passing information to operators didn't mean they had to give away some of their knowledge – they merely had to share it.

In earlier times, an inflexible approach meant that boundaries were guarded zealously. Operators operated machines, quality control staff sampled and tested products, fork-lift truck drivers brought supplies and removed finished products and engineers set, adjusted and repaired equipment. Woe betide anyone who attempted to step over a border!

The Works Engineer found himself baffled by this traditional, inflexible approach, particularly as it was clear that most of the operators were perfectly capable of undertaking many of the adjustment and fault rectification tasks involved. 'Here were people who had rewired their houses, installed central heating, done loft conversions and always did their own vehicle maintenance – but we didn't allow them to touch so much as a single screw on a machine!'

The multi-skilled approach

Under the earlier regime, most of the engineers worked on the plant and were regarded as an élite group with special skills. Reporting to the Works Engineer, they were 'called' to jobs. If an operator encountered a problem with a machine, he reported it to his manager, who reported it to the Works Engineer, who detailed one of his men to deal with it. There were frequent delays, misunderstandings, inadequate information exchange and much frustration all round.

Nowadays, the situation is transformed. Each engineer is an integral part of one of the production teams and whilst he reports to the Works Engineer so far as 'pay and rations' are concerned, his responsibilities are to his team and to the tasks which the team has to undertake. Each production area has its own engineering facilities, stores and workshop, which both reinforces the sense of belonging and avoids the need for engineers to walk unproductively around the site in search of a piece of equipment.

All the engineers are multi-skilled and can undertake work in any aspect of the production equipment: mechanical, electrical, electronic, pneumatic, hydraulic. This is yet another consequence of the liberating climate which has been created.

Communications

One of the most striking effects of the climate of liberation which is now in place is the marked change which it has effected in meetings, briefing groups and training sessions. Discussions used to be extremely hard work. Speech had to be almost wrung from people. At first, when the new structure came in, 'we couldn't get anybody to talk in front of other people. They'd do it one to one: but in a group they'd clam up.'

There had always been one or two people around – barrack-room lawyer types – who were 'not afraid of the sound of their own voice', to whom all the others would defer. No one would be willing to speak until these dominant characters had had their say: and by then it didn't matter anyway.

Now the picture is quite different. People are very relaxed about speaking their mind, and there's a much more positive tone to what they have to say. As a result, the receptivity to training and development has been transformed.

Individual success stories

One of the most interesting results of liberating leadership revealed here is the extent to which individuals have achieved success because of the new open climate. A number of people have been encouraged to pursue personal learning in partnership with the company. Whereas in the past they would only attend courses if the company paid and gave them time off, now they are willing to go to evening classes in their own time, with the company paying the fees only.

Several people have improved their knowledge and expertise in this way and are now making good progress within the factory, instead of being stuck in a role that offered little hope of advancement. In particular, the more open and employee-friendly climate has made it possible for one or two people to reveal their lack of literacy and numeracy skills and enabled the company to help them.

A positive company image

An additional indication that here is a company practising liberating leadership in a comprehensive way is provided by the welcome pack which visitors receive. This announces that the company is glad to see visitors and provides detailed information about practical details on the site. The travel directions are clear and all the relevant telephone and fax numbers are provided. It is evident that much care and thought has gone into the preparation of the pack and the language is friendly and helpful. The final injunction to 'Come as a guest, leave as a friend' speaks volumes for the style of managerial leadership and the open and progressive climate which has been created in this factory.

The LEADER Profile at work

When the LEADER Profile was checked against the kind of leadership being shown at Constar International, this is what we found:

L FOR LIBERATES

Constar makes a particular point of not blaming people for their mistakes and they have established what they call 'The Blameless Society'. People are encouraged to recognise that they have made a mistake, to review it so that they can put it right and then to seek training to make sure that they do not make the same mistake again. A very useful algorithm has been developed for this purpose.

The people closest to the manufacturing process – the members of the area production teams – are encouraged to take their own decisions, basing them on information they gather and monitor. They know that they are trusted. Full and open communication is encouraged and management listens actively to what staff have to say.

Team members are encouraged to develop new ideas. The plant employs SOPs (Standard Operating Procedures), which used to be provided by management for the shopfloor: now it is the operators and the engineers themselves who write the SOPs.

E FOR ENCOURAGES AND SUPPORTS

The leadership gives praise where it is due and takes care to celebrate the achievements of its staff. Over 50 per cent of the site newsletter (which is named *Starteam News* as a result of a competition amongst the production teams) consists of material written by people on the shopfloor.

There is a team brief every month, when the majority of the discussion concerns the plant and its efficiency. The Operations Director is always very visible around the factory and once a quarter he runs briefing sessions for the whole of the staff on site.

A FOR ACHIEVES PURPOSE

Demanding targets are discussed and agreed on a regular basis. The targets are set on a common-sense basis, aimed at just edging efficiencies upwards or trying to solve a problem gradually. The engineers, for example, set a target for each machine, using past trends as a guide to what is achievable.

Constant improvement is a regular theme and it is clear from a tour of the factory that the emphasis on statistics, charts and graphs means that everyone is made fully aware of production problems as they occur and is encouraged to look for solutions.

D FOR DEVELOPS PEOPLE AND TEAMS

The commitment to learning is apparent throughout the factory. There is now a completely different attitude towards training. At one time, whilst training was requested, it tended to be confined to major (and expensive) courses, perhaps entailing an overseas trip. Now people think through the nature of the problem and how to solve it and then make the following sort of suggestion: 'I've talked to the guy who knows about this and he's willing to run a session for us.'

Breaches in standards of behaviour and disciplinary matters have to be dealt with. The concept of 'The Blameless Society' helps here, however, because it provides for a lengthy and thorough first stage before disciplinary procedures need to be invoked. Ultimately, people have to be asked, 'Do you still want to play this game or not? Because if you do, you'll have to play to the same rules as everybody else!'

E FOR EXAMPLE TO OTHERS

The leadership sets a clear example to everyone in this plant. The liberating leader profile highlights the word 'enthusiastic', but in this plant we ought perhaps to say 'purposeful' instead. Managers clearly practise what they preach, admitting their own mistakes and setting an excellent example to others by their own behaviour.

R FOR RELATIONSHIPS BUILT ON TRUST

First-class relationships, built on trust, have been established, not only within the factory and amongst the production teams and others but also outside the plant. The good relationships with suppliers and customers which exist are a prime example of how liberating principles can underpin the very lifeblood of a business. A climate of honesty, fairness and trust is the soundest possible basis for lasting success.

Leadership achievements

This is an outstanding example of how, by flattening the organisational structure and pushing responsibilities into parts not reached previously, a manufacturing plant can achieve new levels of purpose and dynamism. The benefits of liberating leadership are displayed to good effect here, with virtually all the leadership behaviours featured in the LEADER Profile appearing well to the fore.

CHAPTER 11

Liberating leadership action portrait no. 3: Michelin Tyre, Burnley

Our next example involves a factory which is part of a multinational manufacturing group. In this case, the factory employs a liberating approach on the production shopfloor, combined with a more traditional structure at other levels. The success of the self-supervised teamworking has prompted Michelin Tyre at Burnley to conduct a review of management style and its implications throughout the company.

The factory

The company is the largest manufacturer of vehicle tyres in the world, with more than seventy factories worldwide. The site under examination here produces truck and bus tyres.

The development of people leading to improved performance through greater involvement and awareness has been the main feature of factory policy over many years. In pursuit of these aims Michelin Burnley has come to adopt many of the features of a liberating company.

Change or die!

As the 1980s ended and the 1990s began, a deep recession hit the industry leading to an over-capacity in European tyre production. The viability of the Burnley factory was called into question and an urgent review of costs became necessary.

Analysis showed that labour was by far the largest cost element, but a detailed examination revealed that supervisory staff represented a high cost overhead. The factory had always insisted upon close supervision to ensure the manufacture of a consistently high-quality product, but now the high cost of that supervision was brought into question.

Self-supervised teams

It was clear that the elimination of supervision through the introduction of self-supervised teams held the greatest potential for a significant reduction in costs.

During the 1980s, a great deal of 'people development' had already taken place and many of the old 'us and them' barriers had been eliminated. So the ground was already well prepared for the introduction of self-supervised teams – but the critical situation meant that it had to be done urgently and rapidly.

After announcing the concept, an intensive period of meetings, discussions and training began, leading to a phased programme to convert all the production areas to self-supervised shift teams. This was completed in two hectic years and although it entailed an enormous upheaval and affected many people, it proved to be a very positive period for the factory.

The current organisational structure

The present organisational structure is relatively flat. The upper echelon consists of the Factory Manager and a small group of Heads of Department, who together form the team which runs the factory. Each departmental head has a number of cell managers who supervise the teams.

Production teamworking

Tyre production involves four stages: preparation, assembly, vulcanisation and final inspection. In the workshops there are five teams of various sizes, with three teams working on shifts in any one day. Team members take decisions on any issue and deal with any problem which affects the fulfilment of the production plan.

The teams do not have appointed team leaders. During meetings, different people will lead the discussions according to the subject under review. Decisions relating to the availability of materials and supplies or the condition of the plant are taken by the team or by individuals acting on behalf of the team. From time to time, a team might decide to alter the various responsibilities within the team or the arrangements for making decisions.

Communications

There are regular briefing meetings so that cell managers can discuss a variety of issues with their teams. At first, these tended to follow the management's agenda and consisted mainly of briefing down, so that team members were made aware of issues and developments which higher management wanted them to hear. At the end, if there was time, concerns relating to the team itself could be raised.

Today, those priorities have been completely reversed. It is now the team's agenda which is paramount, and the meeting is owned by the team. Downward briefing still takes place, but it is integrated with the need for the team to discuss the issues that matter.

Team members really welcome the opportunity to talk about any problems that may be preventing targets from being met. Managers comment regularly on the benefits of 'sitting down away from the workshop and discussing issues properly'.

Problem-solving and generating ideas

The quality of the meetings themselves and the value of the discussions within them have improved immeasurably since self-supervised teams were introduced. Issues are clarified, problems resolved and ideas put forward. Sometimes these emerge over a period and may involve four or five meetings, but that continuity in itself is a sign of the maturity with which the teams perform.

Many managers are very pleased with the way that discussions with the team can generate good ideas. As the teams have matured, more and more problems have been aired and more and more ideas have come forward. In one manager's words: 'I used to give them my solutions, but now I just give them the problem and wait!'

The LEADER Profile at work

When the LEADER Profile was checked against the kind of leadership being shown at Michelin Tyre, this is what we found:

L FOR LIBERATES

The knee-jerk reaction of blaming someone for a mistake has been all but eradicated. 'The way you treat a first failure is crucial', explains one manager. 'If you get that wrong and revert to the old style, you've got trouble with a capital T.'

Encouraging those who are closest to the job to take their own decisions is an ongoing theme for managers at the Burnley factory. Even though the production teams have wide responsibilities, it is important from time to time to find ways of reminding people that they must take the relevant decisions. 'We say to ourselves, "how can I prevent you from having to ask me anything?"'

The remaining behaviours in this section of the profile (listening, open communication, trust and the development of new ideas) are all well established in the factory. New ideas and solutions to problems are especially encouraged and are introduced as often as possible, because experience has shown that once a team member's proposal has been accepted it is followed by even better ones.

E FOR ENCOURAGES AND SUPPORTS

Managerial leaders recognise that they should accept responsibility for the actions of their staff, and act accordingly. Giving praise where it is due is more difficult, not because people do not want to give it, but because of the practical barriers presented by the rotating shift system. Individuals may not be seen face to face for some days and the spontaneity of genuine praise can be lost.

The effects of stress are recognised and more emphasis is being placed on how to minimise it.

Encouragement and support is provided in a number of ways, and wherever possible it takes a simple and practical form. One example stems from the fact that any member of a production team can authorise stores vouchers: as a result everyone feels that their responsibilities have been enhanced.

A FOR ACHIEVES PURPOSE

The setting of targets and the consultation that takes place prior to decisions have had their effects on the climate in the plant, but the behaviour that seems to reflect the new outlook most clearly is the increased sense of vision. People have lifted their eyes from the floor to the horizon and, as a result, there is a much greater feeling of purpose.

There is general acceptance that continuous improvements in performance have to be sought and people are encouraged to take the longer-term view by increasing the validity of improvement plans from one to three years.

D FOR DEVELOPS PEOPLE AND TEAMS

People development has been a continuing theme at the Burnley factory, even before the introduction of self-supervised teams and the widening of the liberating climate.

Courses have been used to set the scene for development and enable individuals and teams to step back from their normal routine and see what the ongoing needs and requirements are. As people have needed to take on new tasks, they have been given systematic additional training. In many instances, the use of technology-based training packages has enabled rapid learning to take place and ensured that consistency of skill is maintained both between and within teams.

In any organisational situation, whatever its structure, there is a continuing need for the appraisal of performance and the assessment of development needs. Following the establishment of self-supervised teams, a process of natural evolution led to the creation of personal performance indicators and the introduction of self-assessment procedures.

E FOR EXAMPLE TO OTHERS

This section of the profile urges leaders to 'encourage feedback on their own performance, work on their own learning and practise what they preach'. These behaviours are certainly recognised as necessary, and people are working hard to ensure that they are in place consistently right across the plant.

The 'two-tier' organisation structure, which produces some discontinuity between the self-supervision of the production shops and the progressively more traditional structure that pervades as one moves away from production, means that extra effort has to be put into ensuring that an effective example is set all the way through the structure.

R FOR RELATIONSHIPS BUILT ON TRUST

Ensuring that proper relationships are built up, through trust, is a crucial aspect of the LEADER Profile. Many of the required leadership behaviours are already in place, but further work is planned to enhance these and ensure that the truly liberating climate is 'locked in place' for the future.

In the long term, liberating principles can be made to underpin everything that the factory stands for. A climate of honesty, fairness and trust is the soundest possible basis for lasting success and this is being integrated across the company.

Leadership achievements

This is an interesting example of a hybrid approach to liberating leadership. By eliminating the supervisory role in the production units, exceptional increases in productivity have been achieved with a substantial reduction in indirect costs. The company is now reconsidering the managerial leadership style which it uses in the remainder of the organisational structure, so that significant further gains can be made. When this second phase has been completed, the principles so readily demonstrated in the production function will have been extended to the whole company.

CHAPTER 12

Liberating leadership action portrait no. 4: the IT function at Cornhill Insurance

Our final example shows liberating leadership in action in a non-manufacturing environment. Part of the IT function at Cornhill Insurance has been completely reorganised. Whilst restructuring has become almost a way of life for many IT people, it seems that, paradoxically, when a progressive organisation wants to make changes which are effective and lasting, it finds that there is a shortage of proven exemplars to follow.

A new approach to restructuring

David Taylor, IT Manager at Cornhill, felt that in many cases the real organisational issues were not addressed. He wanted to develop a new approach which would deal effectively with change, provide real business solutions, motivate staff and avoid an undue dependence on the skills of particular individuals.

As a result of the restructuring which was set in train by Brian Kurton, IT Executive, Cornhill split their IT function into three parts: Systems Development, Operations and Technical and Customer Services (hereinafter referred to as TCS).

A circular structure

The TCS Department now has a non-hierarchical structure. This is not just the removal of bits of the hierarchy, or a touch of tinkering here and there: the pyramid has ceased to exist.

David Taylor, as TCS Manager, is now at the centre of a circular structure. Every member of staff in the department has specific skills and responsibilities, and everyone is involved in the decision-making processes. No one is anyone else's boss. Everyone works together.

Within TCS there are thirty-two Skill Teams, each specialising in a particular area, such as Unix, PC needs and analysis, communications and helpline support. Crucially, individuals can be members of any number of teams and involve themselves in a range of different projects. Each person has responsibility for a unique portfolio of work.

David Taylor believes that the traditional tightly structured sections and reporting relationships used by IT departments do not work: structures with much more distributed responsibility are needed.

The experience of the TCS Department is that when individuals are given wider responsibilities, when they can work in a number of different teams, when they are involved fully across the whole spectrum of the department and when they can manage their own time and scheduling, they become very highly motivated. People enjoy coming to work and turnover of staff has plummeted.

Domains

Whilst there is great flexibility in the structure and individuals have much personal freedom, there remains a need for strategic control. This need is met in a most creative and stimulating way through the concept of 'domains'. A domain is a defined area for which IT is responsible, such as customer services or strategic consultancy. One person in the department is designated as having responsibility for overseeing strategy in each of the areas concerned, and every project undertaken is allocated to a domain. Domains are not fixed and can be altered at any time as circumstances alter. In David Taylor's words: 'It's not what the domains cover, it's the principle behind them and their effectiveness that matters.'

The individual concerned (the 'domain-owner') is responsible for seeing that standards and values are upheld and he or she is answerable to the business on these issues. The relationship between TCS and the rest of the Cornhill business is on a customer and supplier basis. This concept of domains is a clear example of devolved leadership at work.

The hub of a wheel

This highly flexible circular structure, with its teams and domains and individuals, has a centre. Here sits David Taylor, carrying out a role which is very different from that of a top-of-the-pyramid manager, as he explains: 'My job is more to do with motivation and leadership than management.'

He still has a responsibility for overseeing TCS, but he has no more authority over individual projects than anyone else has. Democratisation has given Cornhill a powerful weapon in the fight to develop and maintain cost-effective IT.

Auditing the skills

One of the keys to the success of the new way of working has been to review and document the skills which the department owns. A clear and comprehensive skills database is being established which will enable everyone to understand the skills which are available, to identify any gaps or deficiencies which need to be tackled and, above all, to utilise the appropriate skill in the appropriate place at the appropriate time.

David Taylor believes that there can be no substitute for a skills-based approach, but, he cautions: 'It's the application of the skills that's crucial'. By documenting the *applicable* skills – setting out very clearly what people are capable of doing – individual contributions may be maximised and a more effective use of resources can be achieved.

This skills database will be developed across the whole of IT, providing the company with an invaluable picture of the technical, behavioural and, increasingly, specialised skills which individuals may possess but which have hitherto remained hidden or been disregarded. Many individuals have interests outside their job which utilise particular skills which could have an application within their job.

Your own personal manager

Cornhill's liberating approach extends to personnel issues. Everyone in TCS has their own personal manager who deals with matters such as salary, terms and conditions and career development.

This remarkable approach ensures that work issues are separated from people issues in a constructive way, whilst allowing the department to recognise the importance of both and to give full and proper consideration to them.

A living and growing CV

David Taylor believes in the prime importance of individuals and that it is essential to develop their potential to the limit. This philosophy is prompted not so much by a need simply to retain people within the company, but stems from the belief that by maximising their potential, people will find their most effective role, both for the organisation and for themselves.

All staff are encouraged to maintain a live, continuously updated CV, which lists their developing skills and indicates successes and achievements. David Taylor thinks that it is wrong for organisations to be very interested in CVs during recruitment and then appear to lose interest completely after someone has been employed. 'We need to consider ourselves not as a current employer, but as a potential employer.'

The LEADER Profile at work

When the LEADER Profile was checked against the kind of leadership being shown in the TCS Department at Cornhill Insurance, this is what we found:

L FOR LIBERATES

All the behaviours under this heading are in evidence: listening to staff, full and open communication, trust, receptiveness to new ideas and encouraging those nearest to the task to take decisions. Above all, however, the behaviour which stands out when the new approach is contrasted with the older style is the determination to maintain a 'no blame' environment. David Taylor is wholly wedded to the liberating concept that regards mistakes as learning opportunities, rather than as excuses for blame and recrimination.

E FOR ENCOURAGES AND SUPPORTS

The 'circular' structure and the fact that a given individual takes different roles in different project teams makes it easier to provide help and support. The absence of a hierarchy and the separation of people and projects means that mutual assistance and support are freely available without the complications of status or power play.

Giving praise without embarrassment and showing people that you have faith in them has become a way of life since the new approach was adopted. It is noticeable that whilst members of staff are strongly committed to the company and to the technology, their strongest commitment is to each other.

A FOR ACHIEVES PURPOSE

The setting of objectives and regular consultation has changed the atmosphere in the office. There is a genuine feeling that everyone is pulling in the same direction. In addition, there seems to be a clearer vision, so that people come to work with a much greater sense of purpose.

D FOR DEVELOPS PEOPLE AND TEAMS

People development is a very strong theme in TCS at Cornhill and this is reflected in a discernible groundswell of motivation. People feel that they are developing and making progress personally, whilst at the same time remaining part of a strong and well-integrated team. Since, in addition, they feel that their individual needs are not being neglected, they feel more relaxed about their work and much more motivated. There is a close link between stability and effectiveness.

E FOR EXAMPLE TO OTHERS

The interlinked matrix in which people work, with a given individual occupying both 'senior' and 'junior' roles according to the needs of the project, encourages a flexible and friendly approach in which each person can act as an example to the others regarding some part of the process.

R FOR RELATIONSHIPS BUILT ON TRUST

Ensuring that proper relationships are built up, through trust, is a crucial requirement for Cornhill. All the relevant leadership behaviours are strongly in evidence: self-interest is outlawed, promises are kept, there is sensitivity to individuals and other people's achievements are not hijacked. Honesty, truthfulness and fairness underpin relationships and set the seal on the democratic work arrangements.

Leadership achievements

This is yet another (and different) example of the many approaches to liberating leadership that can be taken. The circular 'wheel' structure, with the domains and project teams, is effective and clearly right for the nature of the work. The approach is now being extended to all of IT; but this will be an evolutionary process, not a revolutionary one. *Softly softly* and *little by little* are good mottoes for the introduction of this managerial style.

CHAPTER 13

The liberating organisation

Liberating leadership is a concept which brings together a number of new and existing initiatives and binds them into a comprehensive recipe for better leadership and, by implication, better organisations.

Thus the concept of liberating leadership must be complemented by the concept of the liberating organisation. Indeed, since a liberating leader cannot lead in a vacuum, he or she must work as part of an organisation of some kind.

What is a liberating organisation like? What are its principal features? How is it characterised? Such questions are discussed at many different points in this book and the four action portraits, in particular, describe in some detail real-life examples of liberating organisations. In this final chapter, however, it is instructive to summarise all those features which make the liberating organisation so invigorating and mark it out as a managerial blueprint for the new millennium.

Characteristics of a liberating organisation

A flat organisational structure
A flat structure to cut out functionalism, bureaucracy and the worship of status.

Inversion of the pyramid

To ensure that employees who interface directly with customers are supported and facilitated by their leaders and managers. ('Leadership from behind'.)

Organisational democracy

An approach which values the contribution of all and promotes their self-esteem. People are referred to as colleagues, not subordinates. Reporting relationships are less rigid, with many direct and indirect linkages. Managers and leaders are visible, sensitive, in touch and they really do listen.

A liberating climate

A positive and stimulating climate, created by a liberating leadership to encourage healthy development and growth.

Genuine empowerment

The unequivocal transfer of authority, responsibility and resources to those closest to each group of tasks.

A 'blame free' culture

A supportive culture which seeks to eliminate mistakes by using them as learning opportunities, rather than by imposing punishment.

Self-managed teams

Independent workgroups with the authority and responsibility to achieve their agreed targets. These may or may not have a designated leader, and the leadership can rotate. A coach/facilitator may be employed from outside the team.

Mutual trust

A major component of the liberating style of leadership and the rock upon which all effective working relationships are built.

Ownership
Encouraged and established through shared information, the provision of user-friendly procedures and the celebration of successes.

Vision
An inspirational view of the future which is communicated to all and acts as an organisational headlamp, lighting the path ahead.

Values
The principles, beliefs and standards to which the organisation holds. Departmental values and team values should be compatible.

Communication
This should be open, comprehensive and without hidden agendas. Designed to support tasks, clarifying, rather than clouding the issues, this should take place naturally and without affectation.

Development
Individual and team development is an integral part of working, managing and leading. Coaching and encouragement to learn are second nature.

Innovation
Innovation is welcomed, sensible risk-taking is encouraged and fear has been banished.

Attitude
Enthusiasm is evident throughout the organisation and people see any proposed changes as challenges to be met and managed, rather than opposed.

The transition

These characteristics of the liberating organisation, set down like this in such profusion, make it seem like the New Utopia, and can be discouraging to those who still toil in a command and control organisation with no prospect of change.

There are, however, many examples of organisations which have turned themselves around and adopted liberating principles, using a phased programme to introduce them. The action portraits in Chapters Nine to Twelve reinforce this optimistic scenario.

Organisations which are contemplating making such a change should recognise that there must be a lengthy transitional period in which to introduce the new liberating methods of working.

Such transitions cannot be carried out to a prescribed formula, so we do not provide one. Each organisation is a separate case and it must plan and manage its own changes and the order in which they take place. It should be emphasised, however, that when an organisation has reviewed its situation, identified its needs and formulated its plans, everyone must be issued with a large poster which proclaims the motto *Prepare in Haste, Repent at Leisure*.

A comprehensive programme of preparation, briefing, consultation and training is absolutely vital. The caring characteristics of a liberating organisation which have been spelt out in this book should apply to the process used for its introduction as well as to the body created.

Monitoring progress

When a group or company or factory has carried through the necessary transition and can stand up and be counted as a liberating organisation, it begins to look for measures to chart its progress.

Monitoring progress will have two aspects: the qualitative and the quantitative. The qualitative side may initially make the greater impact – a liberating organisation will just *seem* better. That tabloid totem, the 'feelgood factor', will be very much in evidence. People will recognise, instinctively, that their organisation seems more caring, more open and less tense, encouraging them to work smarter rather than harder.

What of the quantitative measures? These, after all, are the ones that really count. It's all very well for the old place to feel more welcoming and for people to smile more, but is the organisation performing more efficiently?

It is likely that the 'soft', qualitative information will show through